Simmering Through The Ages

by Prof. Roland Rotherham

in cahoots with
Master Chef Simon Smith

Photographs by Sophie Overend

A Steve Brookes publication

www.simmeringthroughtheages.com

Cover & layout design:
Alex Buxton
www.maxstarentertainment.co.uk

Photography:
Sophie Overend
www.sophieoverend.co.uk

Additional photography: p36 Alexander Raths, p50 Barbara Dudzinska, p51 Sharpshot, p88 Olga Langerova, p90 drx, p92 Andy Dean, p93 Victoria Short and GB, p118 Mike Eikenberry, p148 Justin Hall, p150 Springfield Gallery

Copy editor:
Bronwyn Robertson
www.theartsva.com

Published in 2009 by
Steve Brookes, 60 Loxley Road,
Stratford-upon-Avon, Warwickshire CV37 7DR

A CIP catalogue record for this book is available from the British Library
ISBN 978-0-956414-50-2

Printed in Slovenia on behalf of Latitude Press Ltd.

Dedications

To my best friend, Guy Clifford,
for being just that for most of my life.

To Chris Geere for writing the foreword,
a great actor and even better friend.

To Mark Davies for stroking my ego
when I needed it most.

Contents

Foreword...

Being an actor, if you're lucky, enables you to spend time with some truly remarkable people. So there I am in Utrecht, Holland, surrounded by thousands of people dressed as mythical creatures, wizards and warlords. This was the ELF fantasy fair; an annual event that celebrates all things magical. I was there to talk about *Blood and Chocolate*; a film I'd recently finished working on in which I played a werewolf. ELF was memorable to say the least because of everything I saw and learnt. It was an insight into a world that I knew very little about until the 'Prof' came along to enlighten us all.

Roland Rotherham or 'Prof' as we affectionately call him is the person we should all have on speed-dial if we want to learn anything... about anything. I was very excited the night when Prof kindly asked me to write the foreword for this book. We were celebrating at the end of a day in which I'd seen him and Master Chef Simon Smith cook some simply brilliant dishes at their live historical cookery demonstration. On the menu: herring pie! How wonderful it was to see (the heads and tails popping out of the pastry) and to hear the history associated with what was the 'Big Mac' of the 15th century!

These beautiful handcrafted culinary memories are insightful, they're a little slice of our history and most of all, they are great fun. Whether you're about to host an original dinner party, in need of some creative time in the kitchen or just want to experiment out of sheer intrigue, then Simmering Through the Ages is a keeper. It most definitely will be for me. Professor, my friend... over to you!

Chris Geere

A few words from The Professor...

Dear and discerning reader, first let me compliment you on your choice of book and may I also add 'welcome'... to the wonderful world of historical cookery.

This is not, however, an historical textbook. Please view it more as a guide to doing something special for your dinner parties.

If you are a serious historian you will, I hope, find much here to amuse you. Let me point out though that many of the recipes shown herein have been modified to today's tables and tastes, indeed some of the recipes covered, in their original form, would be totally unsuited to today's modern palate.

You will find in this first volume not only the recipes themselves but also a little of the history and periods surrounding the dishes. To know something of the period is to know much of their taste.

All this being said let me finish by wishing you that which I consider to be the most important ingredient of all – have fun!

Happy cooking

Prof. Roland Rotherham

Introduction...

I first had the great pleasure of meeting Professor Roland Rotherham at a dinner party in Bromsgrove back in 2005. Professor Rotherham, affectionately known to his friends as Roly, is an internationally renowned historian who has done just about everything from serving on the back of a camel in Jordan to being a member of the personal staff to Her Majesty Queen Elizabeth II. I can recall being immediately enthralled not only by his tremendous historical knowledge but also with his love of good food and fine wines.

The next year I took over the reins at the Lichfield Garrick and wanted to include something a little different in a forthcoming Literature Festival which was to feature in the theatre's programme.

As a lover of good food and wine myself, I was a frequent visitor to Thrales Restaurant in Lichfield and it was there I met Master Chef Simon Smith. Simon was very keen to explore the possibility of cookery demonstrations at the theatre and I was anxious to give these a very different look. The idea of 'Historical Cookery' performances was conceived there and then.

Introducing The Professor to The Chef started a uniquely witty partnership which has resulted in many exciting public appearances, from Chilly in the Trussocks to The Hunt for the Royal Boar! Audiences are enthralled and entertained as they travel back in time to the Wars of the Roses and taste the dishes used by Richard III and his court which tantalise the taste buds. There's a pudding made using oats, wine, raisins and nettles and not to mention the mouth-watering Norman dish of braised oxtail.

Now this collaboration of two great minds has produced something very special indeed in this volume, which contains over 70 amazing recipes, combining culinary excellence with fascinating historical facts.

Simmering through the Ages is guaranteed to delight anyone who loves good food and wine and enjoys reading widely about both these absorbing subjects. It will also appeal to lovers of history who will enjoy delving into the often intriguing facts behind how our eating habits have changed over the years.

I hope you enjoy Simmering through the Ages with Professor and Chef as much as I have enjoyed being part of this great feast of culinary delight.

Adrian Jackson

Artistic & Executive Director
Lichfield Garrick Theatre & Studio
www.lichfieldgarrick.com

"Nature's bounty, fresh and vibrant. The colour and taste of summer."

Salads

Salads

ow, who would have thought that our ancestors would go for the 'Healthy Option'? Well it's certainly a fact that our predecessors from the Mediterranean enjoyed the benefits that a good salad could provide. From ancient Rome and Greece to Egypt and Babylon the salad leaf in all its glory was a central part of the table.

Obviously their climate contributed to this a great deal but as they spread their culture, particularly in Rome, they brought their dishes with them. Olives especially were widespread as was the attendant oil, invaluable to the Roman. Do remember though our ancient Celt and Saxon forebears did not exactly dash to the salad bar to supplement their diet! Apart from the Indian subcontinent where the Hindu faith has been predominantly vegetarian for centuries, that particular eating habit did not appear in Europe for some centuries.

My own dear son, Tore, is actually a vegan (is there no justice?). I have informed him that had he lived in the ancient world he would probably have starved to death! Tofu and cranberry sauce at Christmas just does not seem to work for me at all!

From Victorian times our tables were blessed with the salad dish, that super little kidney shaped object used for serving, literally, the side salad. I am glad to say that particular habit has stayed. Interestingly, the tomato that features so strongly has had quite a mixed history but more of that later.

Hop Bud Sallet

Now for one from the days of the Great Elizabeth. During the heady days of the Tudors the salad or sallet was often a very elaborate dish and used as table decoration. In fact some of them were even made of inedible ingredients and just placed on the table to enhance the decoration of the occasion. This one is very simple and extremely tasty. Some of my guests have said it is an acquired taste but they still come back for more. Here is a real taste of 16th century England.

Ingredients:

Serves 4

- Hop buds
- Butter

♠ Gently simmer however many hop buds you desire until they are tender.

♠ Drain them and then place them in a shallow frying pan with some butter.

♠ Cook until golden and serve straight away.

There you are, a hot salad!

Chef's Tip

Prepare this only as you need it. This is a dish that needs to be served immediately and doesn't work when cooked in advance.

Columella Salad

Columella was a great epicurean from the ancient Roman period and he left us this particularly refreshing little dish. You may like to try adding a sharp lettuce or rocket leaves as a bed for this; it has a super flavour and will transport you back to the days of Nero, perhaps not Nero, let's try Claudius instead – much more stable!

Ingredients:

Serves 4

- 3½oz (100g) fresh mint
- 2oz (50g) fresh coriander
- 2oz (50g) fresh parsley
- 1 small leek
- 1 sprig fresh thyme
- 7oz (198g) salty cheese, such as Farmhouse Cheddar
- Vinegar
- Pepper
- Olive oil, of course

♠ Place your leaves and leek (sliced) into a mortar and add your cheese.

♠ Crush well with your pestle and stir in the vinegar.

♠ Add your pepper to taste and plate up.

♠ Finally dress with the oil.

Columella also added chopped nuts, very tasty!

Chef's Tip
As the oil is used as a dressing, try using first-pressed virgin olive oil. It's well worth the extra you pay.

Cucumber Salad

Here is another from Roman times. The cucumber was always highly prized not only for its fresh flavour but also for its refreshing properties. This simple salad is not only light and delightful for the summer lunch party but will also make an ideal addition to the picnic basket at Henley.

Ingredients:

Serves 4

- 1 cucumber
- 2oz (57g) fresh mint
- 1 tsp honey
- 1 tsp pepper
- 1 tbsp vinegar
- 1 small garlic clove, crushed

♠ First peel your cucumber and then cut it lengthwise. Use a spoon and scoop out the seeds. Salt it and set aside for 20 minutes or so.

♠ Wash the cucumber to remove the excess salt and slice it finely.

♠ Place the pieces in a serving dish; thoroughly mix the other ingredients in a small bowl and pour over the cucumber pieces.

Super if served with fresh tuna.

Chef's Tip

If you are taking this on a picnic, add the mint when you are ready to serve. Do not mix too early. This gives a better flavour.

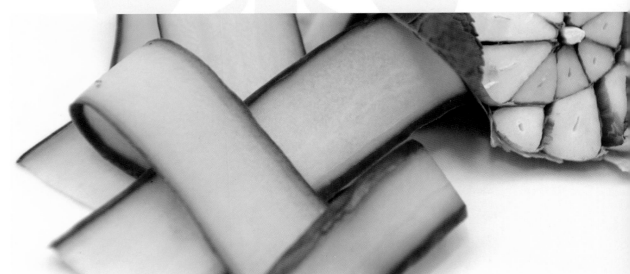

Hen & Caper Sallet

Now here we can go back in time to the days of the Wars of the Roses during the 15th century. Chicken was a very popular meat and used widely. This sallet (salad) was certainly one from the better off tables and makes good use of anchovies. It was not uncommon to mix anchovies and meat during the Middle Ages. The fish imparts a good salty flavour and also a richness that is unique. We must also remember that salt was a precious commodity and using anchovies was a good alternative to the table salt, also much better for you!

Ingredients:

Serves 4 - 6

- Cooked chicken breasts
- Capers, a handful
- Anchovies
- Vinegar
- Sugar
- Oranges and lemons

♠ Slice your chicken into thin steaks and season them with your sugar and vinegar.

♠ Coarsely mince the anchovies and capers and scatter them on the chicken.

♠ Garnish with finely sliced orange and lemon.

Finish off by drowning the Duke of Clarence in a butt of Malmsey!

Chef's Tip

If you can get the large sweet anchovies or even fresh ones, so much the better. If not, the tinned variety will work as well.

French Bean Salad

This particular dish was very popular during the Georgian period. Interestingly, it had become more common during this time for people to embrace vegetarianism. My own dear city of Lichfield which is famed as the birthplace of the great Doctor Samuel Johnson, the legendary lexicographer, was also the home of Doctor Erasmus Darwin, a well-known luminary of the 18th century who was also a vegetarian.

A strange fact but true is that he was also quite obese and his dining table had to be customised with an indentation in order for him to sit close to the table. He was of course the ancestor of Charles Darwin and it was his own work on the origin of species that inspired his grandson.

Ingredients:

Serves 4

- 1lb (454g) young French beans
- 4 eggs
- Juice of a large lemon
- 1 clove garlic
- 2 tbs olive oil
- Salt and pepper
- 6 spring onions, finely chopped

Chef's Tip

Make sure the water is boiling before you add the beans, that way you keep the fresh green colour.

♠ Top and tail your beans and cook in boiling water for 5 minutes. Drain them and allow to cool. Boil the eggs for 10 minutes, shell them and cut into quarters.

♠ Squeeze the lemon and skin and crush the garlic, mix the lemon juice, garlic and olive oil and whisk the mixture vigorously.

♠ Put the beans into a serving dish and cover them with the chopped spring onions. Finally dress with the oil and lemon juice mixture.

This light salad is a delight as a side dish.

White Kidney Bean Salad

Now for a visit back in history to the time of The Crusades. This period influenced our diet more than most people realise. Just imagine being thrust from your home in the shires to the far ends of the world, as you thought it then. The sights, sounds and smells would have been astonishing for the average soldier. Of course, one of the most important things to remember is that they brought the tastes back with them. A real food revolution.

Ingredients:

Serves 4 - 6

- White kidney beans
- Salt
- Sage stalk, (if possible, don't worry if not)
- 1 large onion, sliced very thinly
- A bunch of chopped fresh parsley
- Olive oil
- Black pepper
- Lemon juice
- Vinegar

♠ Soak the beans overnight and strain before cooking in salted water until tender. If the beans are tinned all you need do is drain them.

♠ Add the parsley and onion and season with salt and pepper to taste.

♠ Stir in the oil then add the lemon juice and vinegar.

Chef's Tip
If peeling an onion makes your eyes water, get someone else to do it. It works every time!

Coriander & Pine Nut Salad

Yet another from The Crusades, this is certainly one of my favourites.
Even back in the 10th century the great Saracen geographer Al-
Muqadasi wrote that Jerusalem pine nuts were the finest in the world,
and they are incorporated in this refreshing dish.

One of those strange little facts: the Christian army when marching in
the Holy Land measured about 1 mile across and 3 miles deep! However,
they could be smelled up to 15 miles away!

Ingredients:

Serves 4

- 6oz (170g) pine nuts
- Olive oil
- 1 bunch fresh coriander
- 1 bunch fresh parsley
- Lemon juice
- 3 garlic cloves, crushed
- Wine vinegar
- Salt

♠ Roast the pine nuts in a pan with oil. Stir continuously. Remove when finely roasted and set aside.

♠ Chop the coriander and parsley, place in a bowl and add the cooled nuts. Squeeze in lemon juice and add a little olive oil.

♠ Season with the salt and pepper and add the garlic to taste. Mix in well and add finely chopped spring onions if you wish.

A simple dish, simply super.

Chef's Tip

If you do not have a garlic crusher, use the flat of a knife blade and some salt to crush your garlic into a fine paste.

Rosebud & Gillyflower Sallet

This is so simple. You will see why this became a favourite of the court of Henry VIII. The sallet is light and finely pickled. The effect of the ingredients is to preserve the flowers as well as to impart a unique flavour. In point of fact this is not dissimilar from the pickled salads widely eaten in Eastern Europe. It is possible the idea for this type of dish came from Bohemia during the 15th century and was adapted by the chefs of the period. Either way, this is a lovely accompaniment for a light summer fish dish. Gillyflowers are thought, mainly, to be members of the dianthus family but can, in fact, be any edible fragrant flower. The word "gillyflower" originally referred to scented plants that were used in Europe as a cheap substitute for the spice called clove.

Ingredients:

Serves 6 – 8

- 2 pints (946ml) of rosebuds
- 2 pints (946ml) of gillyflowers
- ½ pint (237ml) sweet white wine
- ½ pint (237ml) white wine vinegar
- 1 cup of sugar

Chef's Tip

Try this with any edible flowers such as nasturtiums. It does tastes better with time!

♠ This so simple, if you have a large earthenware pot to use so much the better. If not use a large glass sweet jar or kilner preserving jar.

♠ Mix together your rosebud and gillyflowers and place them in your jar. Pour in the wine and vinegar and then add the sugar. Stir well until mixed well.

♠ Seal tightly and leave for at least 1 week, longer if possible. This will last for months.

Think of it as a fragrant rumtopf!

Smelt Sallet

Now we can look at a recipe that was used during the days of the English Civil War. From 1642 until 1651 the country was torn apart by a series of wars that left most of the country recovering from this terrible debacle. To look on the positive side, the culinary history of this period is a joy and gives us some truly remarkable dishes. This is one of them.

Ingredients:

Serves 6

- 50 headless, gutted smelts
- 1 pint white wine
- 1 pint white wine vinegar
- 1 onion
- 2 lemons
- 1 root of ginger
- 4 blades of mace
- 1 sliced nutmeg
- Salt
- Pepper
- Parsley
- Lemon juice
- Lemon peel (whole lemon)
- Lemon pulp minus the seeds
- Salad oil

♠ Make a marinade from the wine, vinegar, onion, lemons, ginger, mace and salt. Leave the smelts in the marinade for 24 hours.

♠ Grate the lemon peel and chop the parsley and mix in a little pepper and the lemon pulp.

♠ Scatter this on your smelts and add the oil and lemon juice.

Why not serve with fresh crusty bread as a first course?

Chef's Tip

You may have to order smelts from your fishmonger. Get him to head and gut them for you.

"The treasure of the sea, the jewels of the ocean."

Fish

Fish

Throughout the centuries, the fish course is the one that can be sublime but is also often ruined through overcooking. Fish has been with us as long as we have been walking on the earth. It was probably amongst the first food hunted by man and the fascination of catching fish has stayed with us ever since.

We may certainly assume that in the early years of existence we consumed it raw, after all everyone knows the benefits of good, fresh, raw fish. Certainly during the period we call The Iron Age, our forebears were smoking fish and, indeed, the Celts were exporting smoked fish, cheese and apples to Gaul (France) for many years before the Romans invaded. I find myself amused that in return all we got was the Golden Delicious! Ah well, that's irony for you.

During the Middle Ages fish became a most important dish for the monastic houses in particular. Friday was, of course, fish day, a custom that many still observe to this day. In fact every religious house had its own fish pool in the grounds of, or near to, the house itself. Some of the most superb recipes date from this period and several of them have been included in this volume.

As the centuries progressed the recipes became more complex in their makeup and certainly the ingredients used were of a more exotic origin. The recipes from the 18th and 19th centuries attest to this. Some of the dishes produced at the Royal Pavilion for the Prince Regent by the great Carreme stand as some of the most sumptuous ever created. But to many people it is the more simple treatments of fish that give the most pleasure. It is always important to remember that the flesh of any fish can be easily overwhelmed by attending tastes of too strong a nature.

Salmon Pie

The Norman invasion brought many new things into the country, like rabbits for instance. However, it also gave us some intriguing new recipes to play with. This one, although very simple, is a real beauty. You will be able to see the influence from the crusades in this.

Although Roman Britain was introduced to spices from the East, when the legione left most of the noble families left too, or went with the exodus into the land of Brittany during the 5th century. Have you ever wondered why you feel at home in Brittany? Its simple, they're us!

Ingredients:

- 1 salmon fillet per person
- Softened butter
- 1 heaped tsp cinnamon per person
- 1 tbs raisins per person
- Shortcrust pastry

Chef's Tip

This is a great dish for a picnic served with cold asparagus. Add some tarragon to your mayonnaise for a real kick.

♠ Make these like individual pasties. Roll out your pastry to a suitable size. Place a salmon fillet on the pastry.

♠ In a bowl mix together the butter, cinnamon and raisins. I like to soak my raisins in brandy overnight.

♠ Place the mixture on the fillet and seal the pastry tightly shut. Slit the pastry top to allow steam to escape.

♠ Brush with egg wash and bake for 30 minutes in a medium oven, 180°C.

Served hot it's great and served cold it's even better on a summer's day with a nice chilled white wine. Treat yourself.

Poached Salmon Steaks

Now here is a little dish that we can trace back to the Elizabethan period, in fact to a book entitled "The Good Huswifs Handmaid" published in 1594. This embodies the superb flavours available at the time and the subtlety of 16th century fish dishes. This is a dish almost certainly enjoyed by that great ancestor of all anglers, Izaak Walton. The addition of the beer was quite common at the time and imparts a richness that many enjoy.

Ingredients:

Serves 4

- ½ pint (237ml) water
- ½ pint (237ml) beer
- 1 tsp salt
- 4 tbs chopped fresh parsley
- 1 tsp thyme
- 1 tsp rosemary
- 2lb (907g) salmon steaks
- 2 tsp vinegar

Chef's Tip

Use a light ale for this dish. Perfect.

♠ Mix the water, beer, herbs and seasonings together in a small saucepan.

♠ Simmer them together for approximately 10-12 minutes. Add the vinegar to sharpen according to your own taste.

♠ Place your salmon steaks in a medium sized saucepan and add the cooking sauce. Poach the salmon for approximately 10 minutes or until cooked to your desire.

Serve either hot or cold with a plain salad. Simply delicious.

Shrimps Bruges

This delightful dish is from the 17th century and would certainly have been available to the young King Charles II during the time of his exile in Belgium and Holland after the Civil War and before his restoration in 1660. As simple as this dish is, the flavours are so superb it will soon become one of your favourites too. If you wish to try a change why not add a boiled, fresh crayfish to the final dish?

Ingredients:

Serves 4

- 8oz (228g) shrimps
- 8 large flat mushrooms
- 6oz (170g) butter
- Chopped fresh parsley
- 1 clove crushed garlic

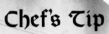

Chef's Tip

When using mushrooms never wash them. If necessary wipe with a dry piece of kitchen towel.

♠ Heat your oven to 220°C and prepare your mushrooms by removing the stalks.

♠ Fill the mushroom cups with the shrimps.

♠ Mix in a bowl the butter, garlic and parsley.

♠ Place the mixture on the shrimps.

♠ Cook for 15 minutes and eat straight away.

♠ For an exciting and exotic touch, add a crayfish, boiled from live, to the dish before serving.

A royal treat!

Rolled Fish Fillets

This dish dates from the time of the Civil War and is of a complex nature. The tastes are very sophisticated as all the herbs used impart their unique flavours. This dish would have been served in a better off household as a delightful Friday dinner. At this time in history dinner was served during the afternoon but we must remember that people woke earlier to start their day in order to make the best use of daylight. Artificial light was expensive and apart from candles the rush light was the most common used – a rush dipped in wax and lit. If you wanted to double your light you lit both ends but, of course, it would burn twice as quickly. Hence the expression, 'burning the candle at both ends'.

Ingredients:

Serves 4

- 1lb (454g) of fish fillets. Plaice and sole are ideal.

The stuffing:

- 2oz (57g) butter
- 1oz (28g) fresh breadcrumbs
- 1 cup of fresh spinach
- 2 tbs sage
- 6 tbs parsley
- 1 tsp thyme
- 1 tsp rosemary
- ½ tsp cinnamon
- ½ tsp nutmeg
- 2 eggs, hard boiled and chopped
- ½ cup of sultanas

Cooking liquid:

- ½ pint (237ml) dry white wine
- 2 tbs vinegar
- 1 tbs sugar
- 1oz (28g) butter

♠ In a frying pan melt the butter and add the breadcrumbs, stirring well.

♠ Then add the spinach as well as all the herbs and seasonings. Mix well and finally add the egg and sultanas.

♠ In each fillet place about 4 tbs of the mixture and roll tightly. You may secure if you wish but it should not be necessary.

♠ Place in a baking dish and spoon on the cooking liquor ingredients, there is no need to mix them first. Crumble the butter on top and place in a medium oven for 15 minutes or until cooked to your satisfaction.

This is superb if you serve it hot with mashed potato that has chopped spring onions whipped in.

Chef's Tip

Always try to use fresh herbs when possible. Dried herbs can sometimes be too powerful in flavour.

Salmon & Asparagus in Pastry

This next dish is exquisite and again hails from the time of Elizabeth I. Salmon has always been enjoyed as a dinner dish and accompanying it with asparagus makes for a real treat, they are superb together.

It would be so easy to imagine this as one of the dishes served to the Queen when she visited the equally formidable Bess of Hardwick at Hardwick Hall in Derbyshire. It is said that when those two ladies met it was a real "Clash of the Titans", both of them extremely wealthy and both of strong character. The dinner offered would have comprised of up to 14 courses. Mind blowing stuff!

Ingredients:

Serves 4-6

- 2½lbs (1.13kg) salmon
- 4oz (113g) butter
- 3 pieces of fresh chopped ginger (about 1oz/28g)
- 2 tbs mixed sultanas and raisins
- 2 tbs chopped almonds
- 12 asparagus spears
- Salt and pepper
- 1lb (454g) shortcust pastry
- Egg to glaze

♠ Cut your salmon into 2 large fillets. Mix in a bowl the dried fruit, butter, almonds and ginger (grated).

♠ Line a pie dish with the pastry, leaving enough for a lid of course.

♠ Place the first fillet on the pastry base and then add your mixture. Top your mixture with the asparagus and then place the second fillet on top. Seal down with the pastry lid and brush glaze with the egg.

♠ Bake in a medium oven for 30 minutes or until the pastry is deep golden. When the pastry is cooked so is your salmon.

Marvellous hot or cold and ideal for that Wimbledon picnic!

Chef's Tip

Don't forget to pierce the pastry lid or it will open at the sides and you will lose the aroma.

Trout & Almonds in Strong Ale

Now for a little something from the table of Henry VIII, or at least derived from one of the time! Trout was popular throughout history and this did not diminish during the Tudor period. There are many trout recipes from this time but this is one of my own favourites.

Ingredients

- 1 trout per person
- ½ cup of flaked almonds per two fish
- 1 bunch of parsley
- ½ cup of strong ale (or barley wine) per two fish
- Salt and pepper

Chef's Tip

When buying your fish, check the eyes are still bright and the gills good and pink. If they are not it is not fresh!

♠ This could not be simpler. Cut out a disc of greaseproof paper or baking parchment about 12in (30cm) across.

♠ Place your cleaned trout open on the disc. Fill your fish with a mixture of the parsley and almonds.

♠ Seal the disc around the trout leaving a small opening to pour in a little of the ale. Add seasoning to taste.

♠ Once you have poured in some ale, finish the sealing of the disc and place your fish on a baking dish and put into a medium oven (180°C) for about 15 minutes. Do not overcook.

This is excellent on a bed of spinach.

Roast Moray

A hark back to the days of Roman imperialism. This dish is still served in some coastal areas of Italy. If you cannot find Moray eel the standard variety will do but the flavour is not quite the same. The Romans used 'garum' as a flavouring, today we can use Worcester sauce instead.

Its fun to think that you can give your dinner guests the same dish that the emperors themselves dined on. How special is that!

Ingredients:

- Allow 8oz (228g) of eel per person
- 4 prunes
- 4 glasses red wine
- 1 dash Worcester sauce
- 1 dash olive oil
- 1 tsp red peppercorns
- 1 red onion

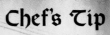

Chef's Tip

Always ask your fishmonger to dress your eel unless your knife skills are excellent. The bones can be a nightmare.

♠ Soak the prunes overnight in the wine, oil and sauce.

♠ Grate the onion coarsely and place in a bowl.

♠ Add the prunes to the liquid and liquidise or pass through a strainer. Heat this mixture gently and reduce by a third

♠ Place the eel in a roasting tin with a little oil and roast gently in a medium oven until almost cooked through.

♠ For the last 10 minutes of cooking brush the eel with the prune mixture and save the rest as a serving sauce.

This is terrific when served on wilted green leaves and with a little horseradish. At least that's the way my guests enjoy it!

Fried Anchovy

Lets stay in Rome for a little while. This is a nice little rustic dish that anyone could do. Anchovies were readily available and certainly nowhere near as expensive as they are today!

For this dish you will need whole fresh anchovies. Ask your fishmonger to obtain them for you. They should be large and plump, similar to the ones served as breakfast dishes in Sweden. Absolutely amazing!

The ingredients are few and the method is simple, as you would expect from a country dish.

Ingredients:

- Anchovies: the amount is up to you
- 2 eggs per person
- Dash of Worcester sauce
- Dash of olive oil
- ½ glass red wine
- Black pepper

♠ Add the oil, wine and sauce to a frying pan and gently bring to the boil.

♠ In a bowl place the anchovies and eggs (having beaten them first) and mix gently together.

♠ When the liquid is gently boiling add the egg/anchovy mixture.

♠ Cook gently and when the anchovies start to brown turn the dish over and cook on the reverse gently for a further 3 to 5 minutes.

Terrific with nice fresh crusty bread!

Chef's Tip

This makes a lovely breakfast dish and will wipe out a hangover in minutes! It can also be used as an accompaniment to another fish dish.

Fish

Baked Carp

This dish was extremely popular throughout the late medieval period and well into the 17th century. Carp was a staple for centuries and its diversity was well known. The flesh of the carp is meatier than most fresh water fish and lends itself well to many dishes.

This type of dish would have been served as part of the multi-courses for the main dishes on the table. It would have been common if entertaining nobility to your home to have as many as twelve or fifteen different fish dishes to choose from. Surprisingly there was little waste as the servants were allowed table leavings and would also have sold them off in the local village. The first 'takeaway' service!

Ingredients:

Serves 3-4

- 1 large carp
- Sweet marjoram
- Thyme
- Parsley
- Rosemary
- 4 small onions
- 1 dozen oysters
- 6 anchovy fillets
- 1 bottle of claret
- 8 cloves
- The rinds of 1 lemon and 1 orange

♠ Place your carp into a large deep dish and stuff the fish with the herbs and onions.

♠ Pour the wine onto the fish and lay the anchovies and cloves around it.

♠ Cover the fish tightly and bake in a pre-heated medium oven for about 30 minutes or until the fish is cooked.

Serve piping hot and with a fresh green salad.

Chef's Tip

Get your fishmonger to descale the carp as this can be a particularly messy affair unless you are used to it.

Herring Pie

This is a recipe I found in a medieval monastic cookery book from Germany. It dates from the 15th century and certainly squashes any rumours that monks had a harsh diet. It is very similar to a Stargazy Pasty but with certain variations.

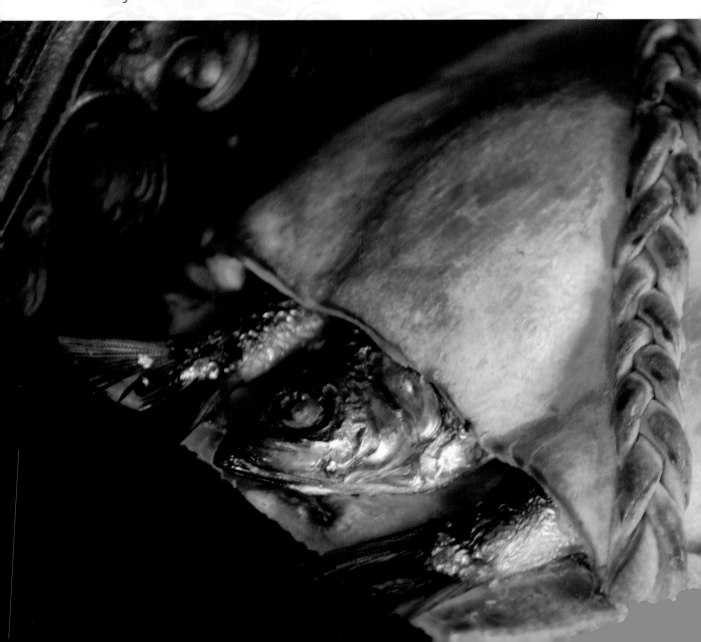

Ingredients:

Serves 4

- 4 good sized herrings, with heads and tails intact
- 2 eggs
- 1 cup of diced, smoked, fatty bacon
- 1 lemon
- 1 medium onion
- A good handful of spinach
- Enough shortcrust pastry

Chef's Tip

Make sure that the pastry is well sealed around the heads and tails of your fish or you run the risk of the dish drying out.

♠ Leaving on the heads and tails, clean and fillet your fish.

♠ Finely chop the onion. Grate the rind from the lemon and save the juice freshly squeezed.

♠ Boil the eggs until firm but not too hard and chop finely.

♠ Line a baking dish with half your pastry. Lay the fish in the pastry and top them with the onion, egg, bacon and lemon zest, and finally top it all off with a layer of wilted spinach.

♠ When placing the pastry lid on make sure that the heads and tails of the fish stick out of the pastry. Bake at 190°C for around 30 minutes.

This is a real winner for a supper dish and is super with a green salad and fried potatoes.

Sardines Stuffed with Nuts

Lets pay a visit to ancient Greece, did they really spend all day running around in little leather skirts? Ah well, I expect it's the sun.

As with Rome, the whole area of the Adriatic was vibrant with fresh fruit, vegetables and fish. This a super little dish that's ideal for the barbeque. Just think that after a night with these little beauties and a few glasses of retsina you can all get the local train and lay siege to Troy!

Ingredients:

- 4 fresh sardines per person
- 1 tsp ground cumin
- 1 tsp ground peppercorns
- 1 tsp chopped fresh mint
- 1 tsp ground almonds
- 2 tsp honey

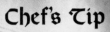

Chef's Tip

To remove the backbone from a fresh sardine simply place it on its belly after cleaning and run your thumb down the back of the fish. The backbone will come straight out.

♠ Mix the herbs in a bowl with the honey and make a paste, add the almonds and stir well.

♠ Clean your sardines and remove the backbones.

♠ Fill the sardine cavity with the herb/honey mixture and gently close.

♠ These will take no more than 5 minutes on each side, whether cooking on a barbeque or under a conventional oven's grill.

If you want to try something different use these fish as a filling to vine leaves. The nut and honey stuffing makes it a great treat.

Lax Pudding

Another supper dish from 19th century Sweden. Obviously fishing has long been a mainstay of the Scandinavian diet. It's all those fjords!

This delight makes use of smoked salmon and dill with new potatoes, a wondrous combination. Many people have asked me why Sweden does not go in for the more heavily spiced foods such as the British favourite, the curry. The answer is simple, the Swedish area of dominance never included countries that had a spiced diet. It was our involvement with India and the East Indies that gave us our favourites; not all countries were such huge pirates!

Ingredients:

Serves 6

- 10oz (284g) new potatoes
- 2 tbs butter
- 1 finely sliced leek
- 10 slices smoked salmon
- 2 heaped tsp fresh chopped dill
- 2 eggs
- 1 cup milk
- 3 tbs double cream
- Salt and pepper to taste

Chef's Tip
You may brush the dish with melted butter, this will give a super topping.

- ♠ Boil the potatoes for 20 minutes until cooked.

- ♠ In a frying pan sauté the leek in the butter.

- ♠ Pre-heat the oven to 180ºC.

- ♠ Slice the potatoes not too thinly. Take a well-greased terrine dish and place a layer of the potatoes on the bottom, top with the leek, a light sprinkling of salt, pepper, dill and finally the sliced salmon.

- ♠ Beat the eggs with the milk and cream and pour into the dish.

- ♠ Bake for 35 minutes or until golden brown.

Tremendous for a real Swedish midsummer dish.

Jansson's Temptation

I am very fortunate in that I spend a fair amount of time in Sweden, a country I have grown to love. The food is not highly spiced but is fragrantly herbed and very flavoursome. Some of their traditional recipes are, like ours, centuries old and still popular today.

This dish is one of my all-time favourites. It is often found served in bars as a supper snack and is even better if made the day before and reheated the following day. The potatoes should be of the waxy variety as floury types can be too crumbly for this dish. I suggest a Maris Piper.

Ingredients:

Serves 6

- 6 large potatoes, parboiled and skinned
- 1 large red onion, finely sliced
- ½ cup of milk
- 1 cup double cream
- 4oz (113g) plump anchovies, Swedish if possible
- 2 tbs aquavit

♠ Pre-heat the oven to 180ºC.

♠ Grate your potatoes and place a layer of them in a well-greased casserole dish. Lay on some of the anchovies and then some of the onion. Season with black pepper and a very little salt.

♠ Continue with this process until the casserole is full and finished with a final layer of potato. Pour on the milk and cream.

♠ Bake for 50 minutes or until deep golden and bubbling. Just before serving throw on the 2 tbs of aquavit.

Marvellous by itself or with cold ham.

Chef's Tip

Swedish anchovies are sweeter and plumper than the English variety, if you cannot obtain them then the normal jarred sort will do but watch the salt.

Creamy Potted Prawns

Now for a treat from the Victorian tea table. Tea time has always been important to the British way of life and the Victorians honed this meal to a fine art form. This dish would be served for 'high tea' which is a little more substantial than its relative.

Ingredients:

Serves 4

- 1lb (454g) shelled cooked prawns
- 4oz (113g) butter
- 2 tsp dried mixed herbs
- 2 tsp sweet paprika
- 1 pinch cayenne pepper
- 2 tbs double cream
- Lemon wedges
- Triangles of hot toast

♠ Melt your butter in a saucepan and stir in the prawns, dried herbs, paprika and cayenne. Cook gently for 5 minutes.

♠ Allow to cool slightly before stirring in the cream.

♠ Place in the fridge until the butter has set.

♠ Serve on the triangles of toast with the lemon wedges.

Perfect for Lady Bracknell!

Chef's Tip

Be warned, this dish should be refrigerated and eaten within 24 hours. It is not suitable for freezing.

"A staple of our diet
for centuries past."

Meat

For as long as we know, man has enjoyed meat as part of his staple diet. Our earliest ancestors would have hunted to bring back the fare for the table long before we became farmers. However, the variety of meats consumed by us is truly astonishing, as is the selection of body parts we choose to eat. I have always stated the bravest person in the history of the world is the first person who uttered the words "I wonder if I can eat that"!

If we look at our modern table some of the offerings are truly astonishing. Who had the original thought of eating tripe? Or even brains and kidneys? And the addition of suet into a sweet pudding would, surely, boggle our minds but no, these are not only accepted but are part of our daily lives.

The Medieval times and the Tudors certainly had a plethora of meat dishes in their diet. During one particular dinner in Elizabethan times we find listed the following in a startling menu of extravagance. I must warn all vegetarians this is not for the faint-hearted.

Roast beef, salted beef, veal, leg of mutton, turkey (a new addition), boiled capon, chicken with leeks, partridge, pheasant, larks, quails, snipe and woodcock. The fish course was: salmon, sole, turbot, eel, whiting, pike, lobster and crayfish. Amongst other delicacies were rabbit, hares, marrow on toast, artichokes, asparagus, turnips, peas, cucumbers and olives. It did not end there! The puddings are listed as: quince pie, almond tart, varied fruit tarts, strawberries and cream and a selection of cheeses. Remarkable!

It is worth noting that our habit of eating cheese after dinner comes from the Medieval period as it was thought that cheese "closed the stomach" and helped the preceding food to settle better.

Roast Bullock's Heart

An Elizabethan dish that would have been popular in the counties. This is certainly a country dish and a most filling one. If you cannot get bullock's heart you may use ox and adjust the quantities accordingly. Even the Romans ate animal hearts, they are so tasty and lean. It is no surprise that filling dishes like this one proved so popular.

Ingredients:

Serves 4

- 1 bullock's heart or ½ an ox heart
- 4oz (113g) streaky bacon rashers
- 1 tsp each of thyme and parsley, dried is fine
- 1oz (28g) shredded suet
- ½ tsp anchovy essence
- Salt, pepper and grated nutmeg to taste
- 2oz (57g) soft white breadcrumbs
- 1 egg
- 1 good knob of beef dripping
- 1 cup of red wine
- Flour for thickening, optional

♠ Prepare your heart by cutting away any fat and all the tubes and membranes.

♠ Mix together your herbs with the suet, anchovy essence, seasoning and breadcrumbs. Beat the egg and add it to your stuffing mixture.

♠ Grease a deep casserole dish and stuff the heart cavities with half the stuffing before placing the heart in the casserole with the dripping.

♠ Cover the heart with the remaining stuffing mix and seal the casserole lid well before roasting at 150ºC for 2-3 hours. Check after 1 hour to ensure the dish does not cook dry.

A real winter warmer and very tasty.

Chef's Tip

If using ox heart remember the flavour will be stronger.

Meat & Herb Pie

Back in time now, to the days of The Crusades. This would certainly have kept our boys well fed during the siege of Antioch. The idea of a pie in the Middle East might seem strange but always bear in mind the 'Brits Abroad' attitude. Whilst having to use available ingredients the concept of this was a taste of home. Now be honest, when abroad haven't you yearned for a good cup of tea? That's a good point actually, why can no-one but us make it properly?

Ingredients:

Serves 4

Pastry:

- 3 cups plain flour
- 2 eggs
- 1 tsp salt
- ½ cup olive oil
- ½ cup water

Filling:

- One third cup olive oil
- 3 cloves chopped garlic
- 2 coarsely chopped onions
- 2 lb (907g) minced lamb (you can use any meat)
- 1 cup of fresh mixed herbs: parsley, rosemary, sage
- 1 cup red wine
- 3 eggs

♠ Prepare your pastry as normal and place in a bowl to prove and rest.

♠ To prepare the filling, sauté the garlic and onion in the olive oil until brown. Add the meat and brown well.

♠ Add your herbs and wine and reduce until the wine has been consumed by half. Allow to cool before mixing in the eggs.

♠ Line a pie dish with the pastry and fill with your pie mixture and use an egg wash to glaze. Place your pastry lid on top and bake at 180ºC until the pastry is golden.

A perfect pie either hot or cold, and super with a good green salad.

Chef's Tip

When ordering your lamb from the butcher ask him to trim off any excess fat if you are going to mince the meat yourself. Too much fat can result in a soggy filling.

Lamb with Broad Beans & Artichokes

Staying in The Holy Land, I thought it might be pleasant to visit Saladin's camp for a couple of recipes. The Saracens had a much better command of the idea regarding a balanced diet than the crusading army I'm afraid. Fish, meat, vegetables, fresh fruit, you name it, but then... they were eating at home!

Ingredients:

Serves 4

- 1 shoulder of lamb or 1lb (454g) minced lamb if you wish
- ½ cup olive oil
- 1 tsp saffron
- 5 crushed garlic cloves
- Salt and black pepper
- 1 pickled lemon
- 5 artichokes
- 10 almonds, green if possible
- 2lbs (907g) broad beans

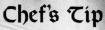

Chef's Tip

If you cannot find pickled lemons you can make your own by filling a large jar with lemons and topping it up with a strong brine. Steep for up to 1 week or longer.

♠ Sauté the lamb in the olive oil and add the saffron, salt, pepper and garlic.

♠ Cook through until the lamb is tender. If you use cubes of lamb this will be about 1½ hours.

♠ Rinse the pickled lemon and allow it to soak in clean water for 20 minutes.

♠ Prepare the artichokes and quarter them. Add these together with the almonds to the meat and mix in well. Add the beans and lemon, sliced, and cook until the beans are tender.

This super Saracen feast is simply scrumptious and can be served with flat bread, pittas or naan.

Lamb Scheherazade

This recipe is rather exciting as it was discovered by a colleague of mine in a Medieval book in Istanbul. Together we managed to translate it and piece the recipe together from the description found. It is possible that this dish has not been widely cooked since the 15th century. How super! A real taste of the Middle East from the Middle Ages! The name of the dish was not shown – Scheherazade is my contribution, after the fictional sultan's wife who narrated *The Thousand and One Nights*. I hope you don't mind.

Ingredients:

Serves 4

- 1lb (454g) of minced or finely sliced lamb
- 4 tamarinds (if dried reconstitute overnight)
- 1 cup of pitted dates
- 6 cloves crushed garlic
- 1 cup olive oil
- 2 lemons, zest and juice
- Salt and pepper
- Fresh parsley, 1 large bunch

♠ Add the oil to a pan and stir in the meat and seal well until browned.

♠ Add the salt and pepper to taste.

♠ Finely chop the tamarinds and dates and add them to the mixture, also add the garlic and stir well.

♠ Cook the dish until the meat is thoroughly done then add the lemon juice and zest. Stir in the fresh parsley, well chopped, and serve straight away.

Chef's Tip
If you find the garlic is a little heavy for your taste simply add more parsley. It acts as a neutraliser.

Baked Calf's Liver

For a complete change I thought we could pay a visit to the young America towards the end of the 18th century. This very elegant little supper dish hails from the New England area and is unusual because at this period of time most European cooks were not using liver extensively in their menus.

Ingredients:

Serves 4

- 2oz (57g) cut macaroni per person
- 1lb (454g) piece of calf's liver
- 4oz (113g) rindless smoked back bacon
- 8oz (227g) veal or chicken stock
- 1 tbs butter
- 1 tbs flour
- 1 tsp soy sauce

Chef's Tip

When making the beurre manié make sure that you heat your butter first then gradually stir in the flour to ensure a smooth consistency.

♠ Cook the macaroni in salted water whilst baking your liver. Keep it under a cloth to stay warm.

♠ Cover the liver with the halved bacon rashers. Place the liver and bacon in a casserole and surround with the stock. Bring the casserole to a rolling simmer and transfer to a heated oven at 180°C. Cook for 30-35 minutes. The liver should stay pink inside.

♠ When cooked keep the liver warm and place in a pan your butter and flour to make a standard beurre manié (kneaded butter), stirring continuously add the cooking liquor from the casserole.

♠ Pour the finished sauce around the liver with the macaroni and serve straight away.

This dish is ideal for a cosy supper.

Forced Leg of Lamb

Bringing our little culinary journey into the 18th century, we can now look at an impressive 'tavern' dish of the type widely found in many of the better coaching houses of England during the days of the powdered wig and highwayman.

Actually, if I'm being accurate, the golden age of the highwayman was the last half of the 17th century with most of the gentlemen being dispossessed royalists from the English Civil War. Do you remember Margaret Lockwood in The Wicked Lady? Is it my imagination or were the films really better then?

Ingredients:

Serves 4-6

- 4½lb (2kg) leg of lamb
- 1 egg
- 2oz (57g) chopped anchovy fillets
- 1 tbs dried mixed herbs
- Grated rind of 1 lemon
- 2oz (57g) soft white breadcrumbs
- Salt and pepper
- ¼ pint (118ml) red wine
- 4oz (113g) small mushrooms
- 4 hard boiled egg yolks
- 2oz (57g) unsalted butter
- Juice of 1 lemon

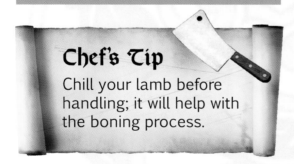

Chef's Tip

Chill your lamb before handling; it will help with the boning process.

A Georgian classic!

♠ Using a long-bladed and sharp knife place the tip between the skin of the leg and the flesh. Carefully cut between the skin and the meat underneath. Separate the skin from the meat but keep it one piece. Again with your knife remove the bone and finally dice the meat from the leg.

♠ Beat the egg and mix the anchovies, herbs, lemon rind and breadcrumbs with the meat. Stir well. Season with salt and pepper to taste.

♠ Place the bone back into the bag made by the removed meat and skin and then stuff the skin with the mixture. Form it back into the shape of the leg. Pour the wine into a roasting tin and add the meat. Roast at 180°C for 2 hours. When cooked remove the meat and allow it to rest.

♠ Make a gravy with the pan juices and in a separate pan sauté the mushrooms in the butter and lemon juice. Pour the mushrooms over the lamb with the gravy and garnish with the egg yolks.

Seethed Meat

Seethed meat is another dish from the Elizabethan period. This super method of serving meat combines the flavours of sweet and savoury that we associate with this period. We often think of fruits and meats together as a modern realisation but no! Here we have another dish from the larger homes of the period. This dish would have been known to the great Bess of Hardwick – that doyen of Derbyshire who was second only in wealth to the great Queen herself.

Ingredients:

Serves 4-6

- 1 leg of lamb
- Milk, enough to cover the meat
- 1 large thinly sliced onion
- 1 tbs peppercorns
- 1 bay leaf
- 1 tbs mixed dried herbs
- ¼ pint (118ml) double cream
- ½ cup chopped parsley
- 1 cup of apricot jam melted with a little sherry

♠ Place the meat in a large pan and add the onions, peppercorns, herbs and bay leaf. Pour the milk over the meat until it is covered.

♠ Bring very slowly to the boil and simmer gently for several hours until the bone becomes loose. Remove from the heat and lay it on one side to cool.

♠ When ready to serve remove the meat, carve into thin slices and place them on a serving dish.

♠ Bring the meat liquor to a fast boil and reduce by a half. Add to this your cream and jam and sherry mixture and spoon the same over the meat slices.

♠ Garnish with the chopped parsley.

Super for Sundays!

Chef's Tip
Dry sherry gives a more voluminous flavour to the lamb.

Pork Pâté

Pâtés have been popular for centuries. This recipe comes from a German monastic cookery book dating from the 16th century. The flavours are intense and this makes an ideal light lunch, first course to dinner, or a super addition to your picnic.

Interestingly many noble houses had small buildings on their roof or garden grounds called Banqueting Rooms. After dinner, cheeses, fruit, wines and pâtés would be served in these in order for the gentlemen to 'entertain' the ladies in private. My word!

Ingredients:

Serves 4-6

- 1lb (454g) of pig's liver
- 8oz (227g) unsmoked streaky bacon
- 8oz (227g) pork
- 8oz (227g) fresh breadcrumbs
- Milk
- 3 eggs
- 1 small crushed clove of garlic
- 4 tbs brandy
- Fresh thyme, parsley and rosemary to taste
- ½ tsp allspice
- Salt and pepper to taste

♠ Pre-heat your oven to 180ºC.

♠ Mince your liver, pork and bacon and mix well together. Fold into the meat the breadcrumbs, eggs, brandy, seasoning and herbs and spices. If the mixture appears a little dry slowly add a little milk.

♠ Butter a terrine dish and fill with your mixture. Place the terrine in a deep dish of water and bake in the oven for 1½ hours checking that the water does not boil dry.

This is super with breads, salad or biscuits.

Chef's Tip
If you would like your pâté more moist, cover for the first hour of cooking time.

Ribs of Beef

Now for something from the recipe lists of the great Georgian chef John Simpson. He wrote a marvellous book called A Complete System of Cookery and in it he shows us many of the dinners he produced at such establishments as the prestigious Guildhall in London during the days of the Prince Regent.

This particular dish could not be more English and it would surely have delighted all who sampled it at one of the great occasions he delighted in. This type of dish would indeed have been served at the prince's great extravagance The Royal Pavilion at Brighton. By the way, the kitchens there are breathtaking!

Ingredients:

Serves 4

- Ribs of beef, a roasting joint
- 2oz (57g) good butter
- 1oz (28g) melted butter for frothing
- 1oz (28g) flour
- Salt to taste
- Gravy as you see fit

Chef's Tip

Always allow the meat to rest before carving, this allows the meat to relax and will make carving easier. For this dish rest for at least 15 minutes.

Serve it with fresh home-made horseradish sauce. Oh my!

♠ Trim your meat of all excess fat. Dry the meat and weigh it.

♠ Allow a cooking time of 20 minutes per pound (454g) plus 20 minutes for the meat on the bone. Place the joint in a roasting tin with the fat uppermost and allow both of the cut surfaces, the side, to be exposed to the heat.

♠ Pre-heat the oven to 220ºC whilst you coat your meat with the butter. Cover loosely and roast as you wish. Remember that blood is a good thing in this dish. The rarer the better, but it's up to you.

♠ Remove the joint about 15 minutes before the cooking time is up and brush it with the melted butter, you may salt it at this stage if you wish. Return uncovered to the oven for the remaining time.

♠ As you slice this meat it will be rich and rare, if you wish, but will also be succulent beyond belief.

Steak & Kidney Pudding with Oysters

Now here's a treat straight from the Georgian era. Let us travel back to the age when Britain was criss-crossed by great roads dedicated to the use of the horse drawn carriage. The most useful places to stop and eat were the coaching inns. Many of these great establishments are still in operation today and still provide succour to the traveller but I doubt whether many of them could serve this particularly rich and delicious variety of what has now become a firm favourite in many homes.

Ingredients:

Seves 6

- 8oz (227g) of plain flour
- 1 tsp baking powder
- 4oz (113g) chopped suet
- Salt
- Stock or cold water (optional)
- 1lb (454g) stewing steak
- 6oz (170g) kidney
- 6 anchovy fillets
- 6 smoked oysters
- 1 chopped onion
- 4oz (113g) sliced mushrooms
- 1 bottle of porter or extra stout

Chef's Tip

When making pastry always wrap in a little cling film and place it on one side to prove for approximately 30 minutes or so.

♠ Mix the dry ingredients into an elastic dough.

♠ Line a suitable greased pudding basin with two thirds of the pastry and press to form a basin shape. Fill with your steak and kidney that has been lightly sealed in a hot pan.

♠ Toss in a little seasoned flour, the onion and mushrooms and the stock/cold water OR soak the steak and kidney overnight in your porter and add that to your pudding.

♠ Into the mix add the anchovy fillets and before sealing with the pastry lid, place the oysters on top of the mix. Seal with the remaining pastry and securely tie in a pudding cloth.

♠ Steam for at least 3 hours.

A Georgian extravaganza!

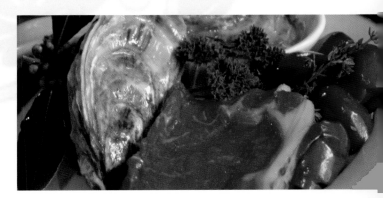

Elizabethan Pork Hotpot

The Tudor period was one of great culinary excesses, even a modest feast would have fed the surrounding population for days but we must remember that simply because all the fabulous dishes were laid on the table you did not have to eat all of them. The amount of waste was astonishing so staff always enjoyed a healthy repast from the leftovers!

Ingredients:

Serves 4

- 2lb (907g) boned shoulder of pork
- A little butter for frying
- 1 large onion
- 1½ tbs flour
- ½ lemon & ½ orange
- 2 cooking apples
- 1 head of celery
- Fresh basil, marjoram and parsley
- ½ tsp nutmeg
- 2oz (57g) each of raisins, dates & walnuts
- 1 tbs honey
- Red wine

♠ Cube your pork and in a heavy casserole dish seal it in a little butter.

♠ Remove the meat and gently fry your onion, sliced, until golden brown. Put the meat back into the casserole and sprinkle with the flour, add the grated rinds of your lemon and orange and their segments. Peel and chop the apple and add to the pot together with the dried fruits, herbs and the celery, chopped.

♠ Stir in the honey and make sure the dish is well mixed before adding enough cider to almost cover the meat. Bring to a simmer and then place in a pre-heated oven at 150°C for 2½–3 hours.

This simple casserole is a real flavour of Elizabethan England.

Chef's Tip

When using pork always try to use free range. The flavour is better!

Pork Pudding

Pork Pudding. Oh yes! The word pudding appears to come from the ancient French word boudin describing a number of sausages used in French, Belgian, Creole and Cajun cuisine. And puddings were normally offal dishes of boiled animal intestines.

Ingredients:

Serves 4

Pastry:

- 8oz (227g) plain flour
- 1 tsp baking powder
- 4oz (100g) chopped suet
- Salt
- Water

Filling:

- 1lb (454g) of lean pork
- 1 onion
- 1 tsp dried sage
- 8oz (227g) sausage meat
- Salt and pepper
- Thick homemade gravy

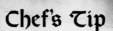

Chef's Tip
The pastry will work better if you leave it to prove in the fridge.

- First for your pastry, mix together the dry ingredients and then work by hand adding a little water at a time until you have an elastic dough.

- Roll out the pastry to about ½in (1.25cm) thick and line a well-greased pudding basin with it. Remember to save some for the pudding lid!

- Remove any skin and gristle from the meat and cut it into small pieces. Mix it with your onion, sage and seasoning.

- Now fill the pudding with alternate layers of the pork and sausage meat and gently pour in enough gravy to moisten well. Seal with the pastry lid and then either wrap in a pudding cloth or cover tightly with foil and steam for 3 hours.

By the Lord Harry! This Medieval pudding is a joy and magnificent for a winter meal.

Spiced Gammon Ham

This magnificent treatment of sliced gammon hails from the 17th century and was widely known in the counties. The addition of cinnamon to meat dishes goes back to the 12th century but rarely has it complemented a dish as well as in this case.

Ingredients:

Serves 4

- 3 slices of gammon, about 1lb (454g)
- A little butter for frying
- 1 cup of chopped celery
- 3 cloves finely chopped garlic
- Ground cinnamon
- Fresh sage leaves
- ½ glass dry white wine
- ½ glass wine vinegar
- 1 cup of white grape juice
- A little flour for thickening

Chef's Tip

Soak the meat in clean water for 12 hours before cooking.

♠ In a large, deep pan fry off your gammon in a little butter until the gammon starts to brown on both sides.

♠ Remove from the pan and place the first slice of gammon in a deep casserole dish. Sprinkle the slice with some chopped celery, garlic, a sage leaf and the cinnamon. Repeat by putting the second slice on top of the first and again sprinkling; repeat with the third slice.

♠ Lightly sprinkle flour over the slices and add the grape juice, wine and vinegar. Place a lid on the dish and cook on the hob until half the liquid has reduced, you will know when this has happened as the meat will literally fall apart.

A sumptuous way of treating gammon!

Spiced Brisket

A taste here of those famous tavern dishes of the 18th century. A journey across Britain by horse drawn coach could take many days and when, at night, you arrived at the coaching inn this would have been waiting for you.

It combines the spices of previous decades but the recipe has become more refined. The 18th century saw the dawn of that which we think of as the restaurant. The coaching inn would become the hotel such as happened in Lichfield at such hotels as The George and The Swan where you can still see the evidence of their coaching origins.

Ingredients:

Serves 8

- 4lb (1.8kg) joint of boned brisket
- ½ pint (237ml) red wine
- 1 tsp ground black pepper
- 1 tsp ground allspice
- 1 tsp ground ginger
- 1 tsp salt
- 1 bouquet garni
- 12 peeled button onions
- 8oz (227g) carrots, peeled and sliced
- ¾ pint (355ml) beef stock
- 2oz (57g) plain flour

Chef's Tip
If you add a good knob of butter to the sauce after reducing it will add a super glaze.

♠ Prepare the marinade by putting in a shallow dish the wine, spices, salt, vegetables and bouquet garni.

♠ Put the meat in the marinade and allow to stand overnight; baste frequently.

♠ Preheat the oven to 180°C. Remove the meat from the marinade and roll tightly. Secure with string and place in the roasting tin. Add the beef stock to the pan, cover with foil and roast for 45 minutes per pound. Baste frequently.

♠ When the meat is cooked remove from the pan and drain, then slice the meat finely and keep warm.

♠ Pour the cooking juices into a jug and allow to stand for a few minutes. Remove any fat that forms and stir it into the roasting pan.

♠ Blend in the flour stirring continuously and add 1½ pints of your cooking stock.

♠ Boil briskly to reduce by about a third. Place the cooked carrots and onions around the meat slices and pour on the sauce.

Excellent when you've been dodging highwaymen!

Stuffed Lamb

I must readily admit that lamb is my favourite meat and whereas I like it roasted very rare, this dish dating from the Georgian period cooks for a long time, but the flavour is remarkable.

Ingredients:

Serves 6 (at least)

- 4lb (1.8kg) boned loin of lamb

Stuffing:

- 8oz (227g) fresh white breadcrumbs
- 4 lambs' kidneys, sliced
- 4 tbs chopped mint
- 3 tbs chopped parsley
- ½ tsp dried mixed herbs
- ½ tsp dried sage
- The rind of 1 large lemon
- Salt and pepper
- 3 eggs

Wine sauce:

- Stock
- 2 tbs flour
- 2 glasses of claret
- Salt and pepper

♠ Mix together all the stuffing ingredients and bind with the eggs.

♠ Stuff the mixture down the centre cavity of the lamb. Roll and tie securely. Roast at 200°C for 1 hour then reduce to 180°C and cook for a further hour.

♠ Deglaze the roasting pan with as much stock as you need and add the flour gradually, stirring all the time. Slowly stir in the wine.

♠ Spoon the sauce over the lamb and serve with seasonal vegetables.

A real treat for Sunday lunch.

Chef's Tip
When making the sauce you may even use port, stir in butter to emulsify.

Sir Kenelm Digby's Winter Soup

A good soup, or 'pottage', has always been welcome especially in winter time when the weather turns cold. This fabulous recipe comes from the household book of Sir Kenelm Digby a courtier during the reigns of Elizabeth I and James I. It combines all that is best in English winter cuisine, it is wholesome, warming and jolly nutritious.

Ingredients:

Serves 6

- 1½lb (680g) shin of beef, cubed
- 6oz (170g) boned stewing lamb, cubed
- Some chicken bones for flavour
- 1 large onion, finely chopped
- 1oz of dried breadcrumbs
- 3½ pints (1.67lt) water
- 2 cubes of chicken stock
- Salt
- A bunch of parsley stalks
- 2 turnips
- 5 black peppercorns
- 3 cloves
- 2 slices of white bread with the crusts removed

Chef's Tip

If you wish you can use a boiling fowl rather than the stock cubes.

- ♠ Put the meat, bones, spices, onion, breadcrumbs and the turnips, cubed, straight into a pan of cold water then cover and bring to a boil before reducing to a simmer.

- ♠ Simmer for 2½ hours then add the stock cubes and 1 tsp of salt and the bunch of parsley stalks.

- ♠ Simmer for a further 1½ hours then taste to see if you need more salt.

- ♠ Toast the bread and cut each slice into 8 squares and place them in the bottom of a tureen or deep bowl.

- ♠ Strain the soup over the toast, adding some of the meat. Serve straight away.

Perfect after a winter walk!

Liver & Bacon with Capers

A supper dish popular for over 200 years. This was on the menu of the St. James's gentlemen's clubs for many years. The original Duke of Wellington was said to have been extremely fond of this classic pairing. As was Lord Nelson. In fact there is a small passage in 'The Village' of St James' that contains the house in which His Lordship kept Lady Hamilton. Such scandal!

Ingredients:

Serves 6

- 1½lb (680g) thinly sliced calf's liver
- 8 rashers smoked bacon, streaky
- 1 tbs butter
- ½ cup plain flour
- 2 tbs capers
- Salt and pepper to taste

Chef's Tip

Using the same frying pan throughout makes the flavours more intense.

♠ Place the flour in a plastic bag with the salt and pepper. Add your slices of liver and toss until coated.

♠ Place the bacon in an almost dry frying pan and fry off until crisp, remove the bacon and keep the fat in the pan.

♠ Add the butter to the pan and put in the liver with care. Fry for 2-3 minutes each side so that the liver is pink when cut.

♠ Transfer to the dish keeping the bacon warm. Add the capers to the frying pan and fry off for 2 minutes.

♠ Place the liver on a serving dish and top with the bacon. Spoon the capers over the dish. Serve with creamed potatoes.

With this for supper 'to the devil with the enemy!'

Sweetbreads on Toast

Another Regency classic. Something from the kitchen of the Prince Regent this time. Here we have a breakfast dish that was served at the Royal Pavilion in Brighton. The use of offal was more widespread then than now. I wish more people would realise that in offal you have tasty and inexpensive meat dishes. This one imparts some excellent flavours and I'm sure the Prince would have enjoyed this before leaving for a day at the races.

Ingredients:

Serves 6

- 1½lbs (680g) calf's sweetbreads
- 2 tbs butter
- 1 tbs plain flour
- 1 cup double cream
- 2 tbs dry sherry
- 6oz (170g) finely chopped smoked bacon
- Salt to taste
- 1 pinch cayenne pepper

Chef's Tip

Fresh lemon juice brings out the flavour admirably.

♠ Prepare the sweetbreads by removing any membrane and veins with a sharp knife. Cut into cubes and place in a bowl of milk to soak overnight.

♠ Melt the butter in a frying pan and add the sweetbreads and diced bacon. Season and add the cayenne. Fry for 3 or 4 minutes.

♠ Remove the meat from the pan and keep warm. Stir in the flour to the pan and slowly add the cream. Stir in the sherry and boil to reduce by half.

♠ Serve the sweetbreads on toast and spoon over the thickened sauce.

What a way to start the day!

Stuffed Cabbage Rolls

In the 18th century the Swedish King Karl XII invaded Turkey and this dish was brought back to Sweden by his men. They substituted the vine leaves in the original for cabbage leaves and I think it tastes even better that way. This is a very popular dish at Christmas time or 'Jul' as it is known in Sweden.

Ingredients:

Serves 6

- 1 Savoy cabbage
- ½ cup cooked long grain rice
- ½ cup water
- 1 tbs butter
- ½ tsp chopped dried thyme
- 1 large onion, chopped finely
- 10oz (284g) minced beef
- 1 beaten egg
- Salt and pepper
- Melted butter for brushing
- Boiled new potatoes to serve

Chef's Tip

When rolling the leaves, tuck in the ends before rolling, they will hold the stuffing better.

♠ Remove the stem of the cabbage and separate the leaves. Cook in boiling water for 5 minutes and remove the hard core of the leaf.

♠ Pre-heat the oven to 200ºC.

♠ In a frying pan cook the onion in the butter.

♠ Put the minced beef in a mixing bowl and add the cooked onion and rice. Stir in the beaten egg and herbs and season to taste.

♠ Stuff each leaf with the mixture and roll tightly. Lay the rolls in a casserole dish, brush with melted butter and bake for 40 minutes until golden brown.

♠ Serve with the boiled potatoes.

Just the thing after a Viking raid!

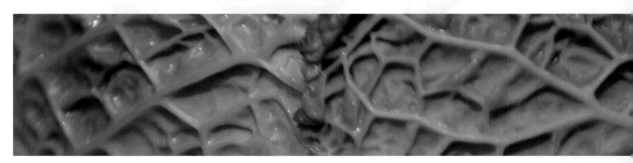

Beef Carbonade

Now for something different. We've travelled back to the Paris of the Second Empire. France was ruled by the Emperor Louis Napoleon III and the beautiful Empress Eugénie. In the days before the Franco-Prussian war of 1869-1870 the great cafés were excelling in dinner dishes and one of them, Maxim's, became legendary.

Ingredients:

Serves 4

- 1½lb (680g) trimmed stewing steak, cubed
- 2 tbs cooking oil
- 8oz (227g) red onions, finely sliced
- 4oz (113g) celery, finely sliced
- Salt and black pepper
- 2 cloves garlic, crushed
- 2 bay leaves
- 2 tsp sweet paprika
- ½ cup chopped and skinned plum tomatoes
- ½ cup finely chopped fresh parsley
- ½ pint (237ml) stout
- ¼ pint (118ml) boiling water

♠ Preheat your oven to 180°C.

♠ Heat the oil in a frying pan and seal the meat, add the vegetables and cook until the meat is deep brown and the vegetables begin to soften. Season to taste.

♠ Place the mix in a casserole dish and stir in the tomatoes and herbs and spices.

♠ Stir in the flour and gradually add the water and beer. Mix thoroughly and place in the oven. Cook for 2 hours or until done.

♠ You may serve this with a topping of sliced and toasted French bread slices that have had gruyère cheese melted on top.

Absolutely imperial.

Chef's Tip

An alternative is to coat your meat with the flour before sealing, which will still help thicken the sauce.

Roast Hand of Stuffed Pork

Once again we have settled in the Georgian era. Pork has always been popular and during the 19th century almost every home that could afford it kept a pig. Have you heard the saying "They put the pig on the wall to see the queen go by"? Lots of people believed that people actually put their pig on a wall to watch Queen Victoria during her processions for her Diamond Jubilee but I'm afraid it's simpler than that. The phrase hails from the Black Country and refers to the people putting a pig of iron from the foundry by the wall to stand on in order to watch the queen's progress. Not nearly so much fun!

So back to Georgian England – it's where we need to be for this dish. This recipe would have been seen in almost every gentlemen's club of the period. Places like Boodles and Whites would have gladly served this to their clientele.

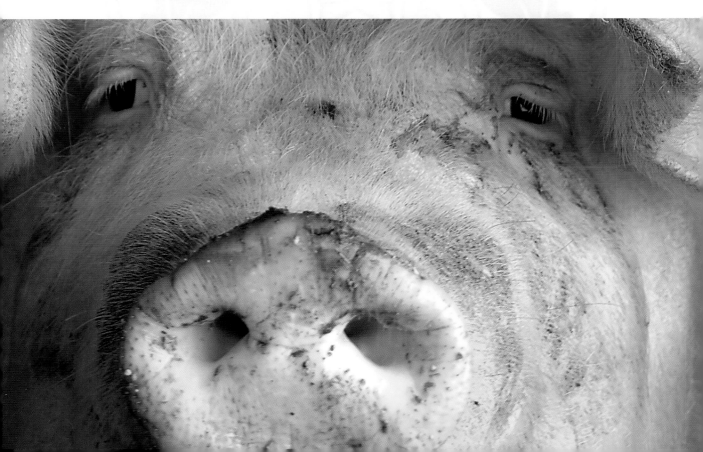

Ingredients:

Serves 6

- 5lb (2.27kg) hand of pork
- 1 cup juniper berries
- 2 onions
- 2 large bunches watercress
- Grated rind of 1 lemon
- 2oz (57g) fresh breadcrumbs
- Salt and pepper to taste
- Ground nutmeg to taste
- 1 beaten egg
- 1 tbs lemon juice

♠ Using a sharp knife with a long blade score the skin of the pork and also cut a pocket under the bone between it and the flesh.

♠ Make your stuffing by mixing together the finely chopped onions with the watercress (also chopped), lemon rind, breadcrumbs, salt and pepper and nutmeg. Bind with your beaten egg.

♠ Stuff the pocket you have made in the pork and then, making sure the skin is dry, sprinkle it with salt and add the juniper berries into the incisions in the skin. Cook at 230°C for 2½ hours or until cooked through.

This is simply wonderful when served with duchesse potatoes and some crumbed green beans. (See recipe on next page).

Chef's Tip
Pork and mustard are a marriage made in heaven. Try one of the new sexy ones such as tarragon or violet.

Crumbed Beans

Simply the only way to serve green beans with the Roast Stuffed Hand of Pork on the previous page and again dating from the 18th century.

Ingredients:

- Green beans
- Fresh golden breadcrumbs
- A good knob of butter

You will never eat green beans any other way I promise you!

♠ Lightly boil your beans. Do not overcook – you want them to squeak. Drain and add the butter to the pan with the beans.

♠ Toss the butter through and then add as many of the breadcrumbs as you wish and again toss through.

Chef's Tip
Always cook your green veg in plenty of boiling salted water with the lid off. This will stop them going grey. Refresh in cold water to stop them overcooking.

Stuffed Dormouse

Now here we have something that you can't try I'm afraid as the dormouse is protected in most countries. I have included it, however, due to the fact that it was so popular and also introduced the dormouse into Britain. If you are not of a squeamish disposition, read on...!

The dormouse was fattened by feeding it nuts before being killed, gutted and skinned.

The stuffing was made equally of minced pork and the minced meat of other dormice. This was mixed with pepper, pine kernels, asafoetida (a plant of the parsley family) and liqumen (very similar to Worcester sauce with olive oil in) to make a smooth paste.

After stuffing the mixture into the skin, the dormouse was sewn up and slow roasted at 180°C until tender – usually 25-30 mins.

There you have it! But don't try this at home – they do wriggle so!

"Man the hunter, with the forest treasury laid bare."

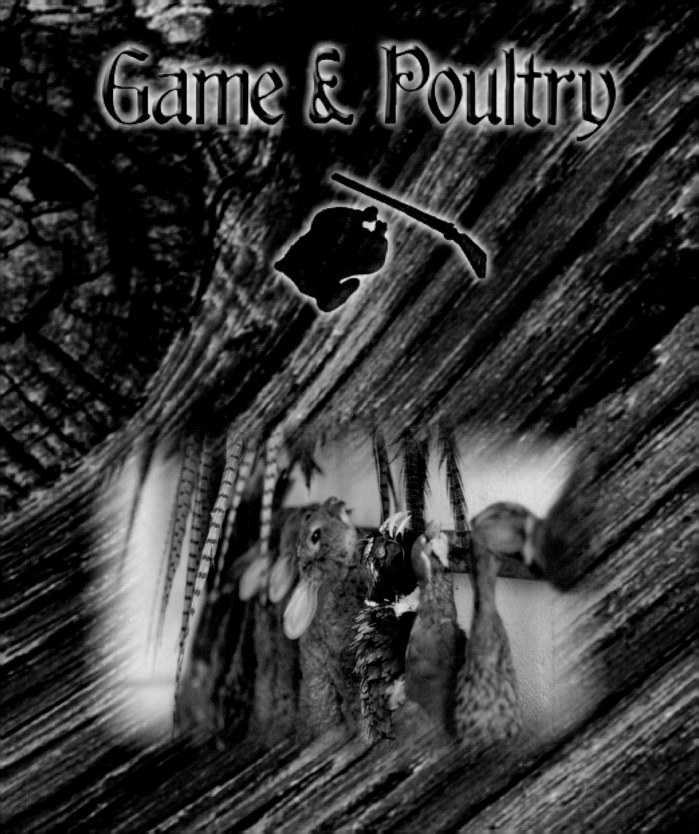

Game & Poultry

Game & Poultry

Of all the courses available to us I must confess a particular passion for game and poultry. There's something about that little hint of fur and feather that can really enliven the dinner table.

Fortunately I am not alone in this and the whole range of game and feathered delicacies has enjoyed popularity for many centuries. Of course we can trace the pursuit of the animals and birds back to our primordial past as hunter-gatherers and many who enjoy shooting now, whether they are farmers or members of a shooting club, are still pitting their wits against the wild in order to provide one for the pot, or in some cases, a few for the butcher.

When you are patrolling your high street for the more rustic of comestibles you will find some butchers who are simply that: they sell mass produced meat in plastic trays that are normally mediocre at best. However, if you look at smaller shops, many of whom are still family owned or only service three or four of their own establishments, you will probably find them proudly displaying the sign Game Merchant on their frontage. Hoorah! You have found Nirvana, not the 'grunge' rock band of course (whatever grunge is) but a supplier of good game that is more than likely served by their own local shoot.

Our history of the use of game is long and complex. In fact during the ages past we have eaten some creatures that have long since died out from our native shores. It was very common for our Medieval predecessors to go hunting for heron to supplement the pot, this was especially popular in the marsh areas and, unless I am very much mistaken, in East Anglia they were known as 'fen splodgers' and the practice went on until the 19th century. Equally strange is the fact that in the South West of our country during the Bronze and Iron Ages and indeed throughout the Roman occupation one of our native birds was the pelican. Certainly smaller than its Antipodean cousin but every bit as scrumptious I'm sure. Do you know I astonish myself at times!

Fowl Rice Pudding

Now for something a little different. This hails from the east of England and is little known anywhere else. It includes the use of nutmeg, which was very common in Medieval times. It was considered by many an aphrodisiac but in larger quantities could induce illusions and even act as a poison.

Ingredients:

Serves 4-6

- 1 large boiling fowl
- 1 cup of rice
- 1 pint (473ml) of milk
- Salt
- Pepper
- Grated nutmeg
- 4 large onions, peeled and sliced
- Bouquet garni
- 1 bunch of chopped parsley
- 4 sliced hard boiled eggs

♠ Pre-heat the oven to 150ºC. In a deep casserole dish place the chicken and add the milk, rice, salt to taste, a very large pinch of pepper, ½ tsp of nutmeg, the onions and herbs.

♠ Cover tightly with a lid and leave to cook for at least 4 hours, longer if you wish. Check on the liquid level and top up with more milk if necessary.

♠ Serve the chicken piping hot with the rice, and garnish with the parsley and eggs.

Simply super for supper.

Chef's Tip

If using an AGA place this dish in the slow oven; if cooking with a normal oven you must keep checking for boiling dry. The chicken should emerge deep golden brown.

Spatchcock Pigeon in Beer & Berry Sauce

This is one for that special occasion. We believe it is possible that this dish originated in Ancient Egypt at least 2,000 BC. Astonishing to think that you can share a meal with a pharaoh. The ale we use in this is quite strong whereas the Egyptian beer would have been slightly more innocuous. The only reason being that over the centuries our taste buds have changed and, besides, I like it!

Ingredients:

- 1 pigeon per person
- 1 bottle of strong dark ale or barley wine
- 8oz (227g) autumn fruits
- Olive oil
- Salt and pepper
- 8 or 10 garlic cloves
- A little honey

Chef's Tip

To obtain a richer flavour you can add a good knob of butter to the sauce before serving; this will give a fine glaze to the dish.

♠ Split your pigeons along the breast and open the carcass. Pierce and spread open with 2 skewers crosswise.

♠ Heat the olive oil in a pan and seal your birds. Season and remove from the pan. Add the garlic whole to the pan and fry gently for 2/3 minutes.

♠ Add half the ale and reduce rapidly. Bruise the fruits and add to the pan.

♠ Replace the birds in the pan and baste well. Add the remaining ale and place in a medium oven for 10 minutes.

♠ Remove and drizzle with honey. Stir the birds in the sauce on a ring for a further 3 or 4 minutes and serve straight away.

A real treat for Rameses.

Venison Blankets

A superb dish now from the reign of James I. He who loved Cock-a-Leekie Soup also had a penchant for good game dishes and it doesn't get much better than this. Venison is, perhaps, one of the most noble of the game meats. The Normans prized it so highly that the penalties for poaching deer were extreme and violent. This method combines my favourite mustard as well – Tewkesbury. It's well worth getting.

Ingredients:

Serves

- 1lb (454g) of venison fillet
- Tewkesbury mustard
- Cracked black pepper
- Butter for frying
- 8oz (227g) fresh gooseberries
- Fresh green beans

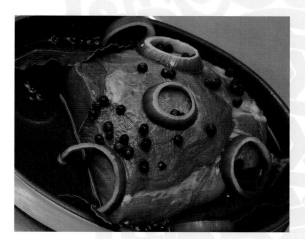

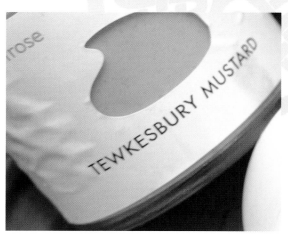

♠ Place your venison in a fridge to chill overnight.

♠ Remove and spread liberally with the mustard. Roll the venison in the pepper and place in a pan with hot butter to seal the meat.

♠ Cook for no more than 5-7 minutes maximum. Remove and rest.

♠ Add your gooseberries to the pan and bruise them to release their flavour, cook briskly to form a sauce. You may add some port to the sauce for extra zing!

♠ Slice the meat finely and lay over beans that have been lightly steamed and tossed in butter and breadcrumbs. Pour over the sauce and enjoy.

Eat like a king!

Chef's Tip
Venison should always be rare and very pink inside when sliced. Avoid overcooking.

Boar & Pear Pie

Staying with the Medieval theme here is a particularly pleasing dish that merges the flavours of boar with that of the finest English pears, a match made in heaven. Over the years people have stopped using fruit and meat together as we used to and I've always thought this a pity. This pie celebrates all that's best in our ancient cuisine.

Ingredients:

Serves 4

- 1½lb (680g) wild boar
- 6 large Conference pears
- Shortcrust pastry
- Paprika
- Salt and pepper
- 1 cup of Perry or dry cider
- Butter for frying
- Egg wash

Chef's Tip

Boar can be very expensive; don't be afraid to use a good quality pork loin for this dish.

♠ Cut the meat into ½ inch (12mm) cubes and seal in a hot pan using the butter. Place the meat into a dish until ready to use.

♠ Line a greased pie dish with the pastry whilst keeping enough back for a lid. Place a layer of the boar on the pastry and sprinkle liberally with the paprika, salt and pepper.

♠ Make a layer of the peeled, cored and sliced pears. Repeat this until the pie is filled.

♠ Pour in your Perry and seal with the pastry lid. Egg wash for glazing. Bake at 180°C for about 40 minutes and serve piping hot.

A real winner for any boar enthusiast!

Mumbled Rabbit

Believe it or not, mumbling a rabbit is not an offence but a delightful supper dish from the 14th century. Rabbits were originally introduced into Britain by the Normans for food and were only for the noble table. After a while though, rabbits being what they are, their propensities made them less rare and soon all were enjoying this delicate meat.

Ingredients:

Serves 4

- 1¼lb (567g) boneless rabbit meat
- Bouquet garni
- Salt and pepper
- 3 hard-boiled eggs
- 2 anchovy fillets
- 3 tbs butter

Chef's Tip

Frozen rabbit cubed is readily available. You may, of course, use this.

♠ Cut the rabbit into small pieces and add to a pan of boiling salted water with the bouquet garni. Simmer gently for about 10 minutes.

♠ In a frying pan heat the butter and chop the anchovies. Add the anchovies to the frying pan.

♠ Drain the rabbit and also add to the frying pan, chop the eggs and stir them gently into the mix. Adjust the seasoning to taste.

♠ Serve onto thick slices of hot, toasted, crusty bread with lashings of butter.

♠ Fry gently for two or three minutes until the rabbit is hot.

You may serve this with pasta, though I personally love it on the hot buttered toast. Oh my, yes!

Duck with Turnips

Our journey will take us back in time to the days of ancient Rome. A version of this dish is still served in some regions of France but this is one of its predecessors. We believe that this recipe comes from that great Roman gourmet Apicius. He left us with many dishes but this is one of my favourites. Duck has always been much loved by the game hunter and it was the same in Roman times.

Ingredients:

Serves 4

- 1 duck
- 1 bunch dill
- 1 bunch parsley
- 1 bunch coriander
- 5 tsp olive oil
- 2lb (907g) turnips
- 3 cloves garlic
- 1 tsp cumin seeds
- 1 tsp peppercorns
- 2 tsp flour
- Dash of vinegar
- 1 large leek

Chef's Tip

The boiling helps disperse some of the fat attendant in duck.

♠ In a large saucepan boil enough water to just cover the bird and add the flour, parsley, dill and coriander. Put in the duck and simmer it for about 10-15 minutes.

♠ In a casserole dish heat the olive oil and transfer the duck to it. Cover with the boiling stock and loosely cover it, boil gently for 1½ hours and add the turnips, chopped, about 20 minutes before the end of cooking.

♠ In a mortar grind together the garlic and spices and then remove the duck and turnips from the casserole. Keep warm. Bring the casserole to a boil on a ring and reduce the stock by half.

♠ In a separate deep frying pan, heat some butter and add the leek and vinegar. Removing the herbs from the reduced stock, sieve the stock into the frying pan. Prepare the duck meat by jointing or carving and add to the pan with the turnips.

Jolly good nosh!

Roast Pigeon with Herb Mayonnaise

Another fine dish from the Eternal City. Even though the ingredients may seem complex it is surprisingly easy to prepare and cook, and makes for a welcome addition to the dinner table. The herb mayonnaise used is still served not only in France but also Holland and Germany. Simply delightful for any barbeque.

Ingredients:

Allow 1 pigeon per person

- 2 egg yolks
- 1 tsp honey
- Olive oil
- 1 tsp lovage seeds
- 1 tsp caraway seeds
- 1 tbs dried onion
- 2oz (57g) fresh coriander
- 2oz (57g) fresh mint
- Vinegar
- 1 date
- 4 anchovies
- 1 tsp peppercorns
- 2fl.oz (59ml) strong white wine

Chef's Tip
If you do not wish to use anchovies, substitute with a tablespoon of Worcester sauce.

♠ Cut the pigeon along the backbone and splay out securing crossways with two skewers. Brush with olive oil and place, flesh down, on the barbeque. Cook until brown and then turn the bird over and cook until done.

♠ Whisk together your egg yolks, honey and vinegar. Next slowly add the olive oil beating continuously until you achieve the consistency of mayonnaise.

♠ In a mortar grind the lovage and caraway seeds. Next grind in the onion, mint, coriander, date, anchovies and peppercorns. Make it into a paste with a little white wine and slowly add this to your mayonnaise.

♠ Serve this with the pigeon and enjoy!

A perfect summer dish.

Chicken Heliogabalus

Staying in Rome (why move, the weather's better!) here is a delight from the Imperial Table. This dish is named after the rather decadent emperor Varius Heliogabalus. Many emperors were known for their vices, and good old Varius certainly loved his food. It is said that gluttony is one of the seven deadly sins. If that is the case I'm sure the other six are far more deadly!

Ingredients:

Serves 4

- 1 boiling fowl
- 1 leek
- 1 bunch fresh coriander
- A few stalks of savory (a herb)
- Salt
- Olive oil
- 4 pints (2ltr) medium white wine
- 8oz (227g) pine nuts
- 1 tsp ground peppercorns
- 1 pint (473ml) milk
- 3 cooked egg whites, chopped

Chef's Tip

If you can't get savory, adding a stick of cinnamon makes for a very pleasing flavour.

♠ Cut the leek in half lengthways and clean out. Make a bundle of it with the savory and place it in a pan.

♠ Put the chicken and coriander on top and pour in a little olive oil and the wine.

♠ Cover the pan and bring it slowly to the boil removing any scum from the bird. Simmer gently for 1½ hours.

♠ Remove half the stock from the pan and pour it into another pan adding the milk, and reduce rapidly to half its amount.

♠ Grind the pine nuts, pepper and oil to make a paste and add this to the reduced stock. Add the egg whites and adjust the seasoning if you wish.

♠ Remove the chicken from its pot and place on a serving dish, pour the reduced stock with the eggs over it and serve.

Simply imperial!

Pheasant with Celery & Cream

Back in the 18th century many of the country houses boasted fine kitchens and it was quite common for the hosts and hostesses to attempt to outdo each other when it came to dinner parties. During the earlier years the main meal of the day was mostly at that which we call lunchtime, but during the 18th century we get the start of what we now know as the dinner party. Many of the finer houses even tempted chefs away from France and Germany to work at their houses. This dish is one that would be have been perfectly at home on one of those tables.

Ingredients:

Serves 4

- 1 pheasant
- ¾ pint (355ml) of chicken stock
- 1 head of celery
- 1 small onion
- ¼ pint (118ml) double cream
- 2oz (57g) beurre manié (kneaded butter)
- Lemon juice
- Salt and pepper
- Lemon wedges

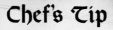

Chef's Tip

Make sure you use double cream in this dish; single cream will split.

♠ Make sure your bird is well dressed and clean inside. Put ½ pint of the stock into a saucepan and slowly bring to the boil. Add your bird and simmer for about 40 minutes until the bird is tender.

♠ Clean and split the celery and cut into chunks of about ¼ inch (6mm), do the same for the onion and add them to the pot 10 minutes before cooking completion time.

♠ Drain the pheasant and the vegetables and keep warm. Pour the remainder of the stock into a smaller pan. Slowly stir in the cream then gradually stir in the beurre manié to make a thick sauce.

♠ Add to this the celery and onion and season to taste adding a little lemon juice as you need.

♠ Place the pheasant on a serving dish and cover with the sauce. Garnish with the lemon wedges.

This is truly a remarkable dish. The Prince Regent would have been proud!

Hotchpot

Here is a country dish from the 17th century. Those who lived in the shires knew the importance of good wholesome cooking that would keep you going. This filling and warming dish would have graced the homes of many a squire during this period. The recipe comes from Robert May, that great epicurean of the restoration whose recipes have been legendary for years. His real mincemeat for Christmas is a joy.

Ingredients:

Serves 8

- 2lb (907g) brisket of beef
- 2lb (907g) boneless mutton
- 2lb (907g) stewing veal
- 10 cups beef stock
- 1 cup chopped parsley
- ½ cup chopped basil
- ¼ cup chopped tarragon
- 1 bay leaf
- ½lb (227g) cabbage sliced
- 6 small onions
- 6 sliced carrots
- 3 large hard apples, peeled, cored and quartered

♠ Put all the meat in a large heavy pot and add the stock, the liquid should be a minimum of 6 inches over the meat. Bring to the boil and skim off any unwanted scum.

♠ Add the herbs and vegetables and simmer for 1½ hours before adding the apples.

A real rib sticker this one!

Chef's Tip
To avoid sticking to the pan, you must remember to stir this dish well from the bottom while cooking.

Rabbit & Apple Pie

Now here is a super little morsel from the Normans, who introduced the rabbit to Britain. This can be eaten either hot or cold and is a delight in the summer. My guests always ask for it if I give them choice of menu. By the way, did you know that England is the only country that grows an apple especially for cooking? It's true!

Ingredients:

Serves 4

- 1 large rabbit, skinned and boned
- Shortcrust pastry
- 4 or 5 large cooking apples, peeled and cored
- Black pepper
- Cinnamon
- Egg wash

Chef's Tip

If you wish to enhance the flavour of the rabbit even more then toss the meat cubes in a little cinnamon before sealing.

♠ Well grease a deep pie dish and line with the shortcrust pastry.

♠ Seal the rabbit after cutting into cubes in a little butter. Layer the rabbit in the pie with alternate layers of apple slices, and sprinkle each layer liberally with the pepper and cinnamon.

♠ You won't need any stock, the apples will cook down and produce their own.

♠ After brushing the pastry lid with egg wash, bake at 170ºC for about 45 minutes or until the pie is a deep golden brown.

Super cold for picnics.

Stuffed Hare

Here we have another offering from the Romans and something that was eaten in Britain during their occupation. The ancient Britons would have shunned the eating of hare as it was considered by many to be the servant of the moon goddess and therefore a sacred animal. The recipe remains, however, one that is truly memorable from the Roman table. The stuffing may seem fussy but it's worth the effort.

Ingredients:

Serves 4

- 1 hare, cleaned and trussed
- 1 tbs butter
- 1 tbs flour
- 1 small onion, diced
- 1/2 cup dates , chopped
- 1 good pinch of pepper
- 1 cup spiced wine

Stuffing:

- 1 tbs pine kernels
- 1 tbs chopped almonds
- 1 tbs oregano
- 1 tbs chopped nuts
- The chopped hare giblets
- 4oz (113g) chopped cooked chicken livers
- 1 tbs Worcester sauce
- 3 eggs for binding

♠ Obtain a length of natural sausage skin from your butcher.

♠ In a bowl mix all the stuffing ingredients, stir and blend together well. Spoon the stuffing into the sausage skin and then stuff the whole skin into the cavity of the hare.

♠ Roast slowly at about 150°C until the hare is tender.

♠ Make a simple roux using the butter and flour, and blend in the chopped dates and pepper with a little finely diced onion and enough spiced wine to make a rich sauce.

Spoon over and bring on the gladiators!

Chef's Tip

Try and gut a hare with the blood still in the carcass. It's great to use it for thickening the sauce and adding extra flavour. Don't prepare this dish in front of the squeamish!

Chicken in Prunes

Another Elizabethan delight from the days of 'Good Queen Bess'. Again meat and fruit – we really should get back into the habit. The prunes used were home dried plums from Portugal in many houses, the Elvas plum being a particular favourite.

Ingredients:

Serves 4

- 1 large jointed chicken
- 4oz (113g) prunes
- Flour
- Salt and pepper
- 3oz (85g) of good butter
- 7fl.oz (207ml) white wine
- 7fl.oz (207ml) prune juice
- 7fl.oz (207ml) chicken stock
- 1 red pepper
- 1 onion
- A few strips of lemon rind
- A bunch of fresh chopped parsley

Chef's Tip

If using dried prunes add some extra flavour and juiciness by soaking them overnight in some alcohol, particularly brandy. This will plump them up and they soak up much of its flavour.

♠ Allow your prunes to soak in boiling water overnight before cooking this dish. Actually you can also soak in brandy (guess what I do!)

♠ Pre-heat the oven to 180ºC.

♠ Coat the chicken pieces in the flour seasoned with salt and pepper, and cook in hot butter until golden brown. Put the joints into a casserole dish.

♠ Fry off strips of the pepper and onion and add to the chicken. In the frying pan add the remaining seasoned flour to all the liquid ingredients and blend until thickened and smooth.

♠ Add this stock with the lemon rind and parsley to the chicken and prunes and cook for 2 hours.

Chicken and prunes, a 'regular' treat!

Braised Elk with Juniper Berries

How Norse can you get? Elk is very popular in Sweden as it is a readily available game meat. This recipe is at least four hundred years old and contains much of that which made Swedish food so enjoyable. Interestingly elk can only be shot by a licensed elk hunter. Whereas many people hunt and shoot you have to pass a special test when going after elk. When hunting you can still be surprised by wolves and bears – very exciting and this is just the meal for afterwards.

Ingredients:

Serves 6

- 3lbs (1.36kg) elk meat, diced
- 2 tbs butter
- 1 tbs oil
- 1 onion, chopped
- 1 carrot, chopped
- 2 celery sticks, chopped
- 1 cup red wine
- 1 tbs blackberry jelly or jam
- 10 crushed juniper berries
- 1 sprig fresh thyme
- 1 bay leaf
- 2 cups water
- 1 tbs plain flour
- 1 cup double cream
- Salt and pepper to taste
- Pickled cucumber for serving

Chef's Tip
In Britain you may substitute venison for elk.

♠ Heat the oil and 1 tablespoon of butter in a heavy pan. Add the elk or venison and fry for 15 minutes until deep brown.

♠ Add the onion, carrot, celery, red wine, jam, juniper berries, thyme, bay leaf, salt and pepper and bring to the boil and reduce by half.

♠ Add the water and simmer for 40 minutes or until the meat is tender.

♠ Strain the meat onto a dish and keep warm.

♠ In a saucepan make a roux from the remaining butter and flour and gradually add the cooking stock.

♠ Boil briskly and reduce by half.

♠ You may add more butter to glaze the sauce if you wish. Pour over the meat and garnish with the pickled cucumber.

A stunning supper dish.

"The perfect end
to a perfect meal."

Puddings & Cakes

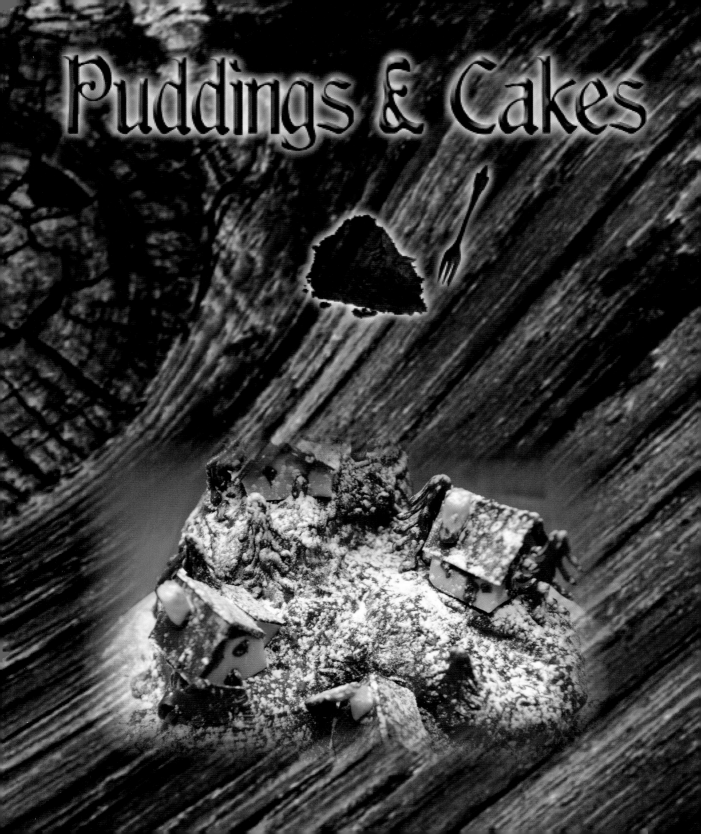

Puddings & Cakes

In this last section I can really indulge myself. I make no illusions to the fact I love puddings! And why not? The variety is simply endless and they have been with us for thousands of years.

As I mentioned in the text earlier, puddings are originally animal offal boiled in the intestines or stomach bag of the animal, but as our ancestors experimented with flavours so the sweet pudding came into being. As the years progressed the pudding, instead of just being boiled became the all-encompassing name of the sweet course served towards the end of the meal.

The Middle Ages gave us some excellent dishes such as the cawdle that I shall commence with and yet was not a pudding as we know it; although it makes an excellent sweet choice it was actually served as a breakfast dish. Over the centuries however our taste buds have changed from the original devices of these dishes and we must adjust accordingly. I have in my collection a recipe from Michel De Nostradame, known better as Nostradamus. His recipe for quince jelly was ideal for the 15th century but today is almost inedible as it is nearly crystalline with sugar. Few know that apart from his prophecies he was also a practising doctor of medicine and a very enthusiastic amateur cook.

During the 16th century huge sugar sculptures were made to adorn a table but were never actually eaten. Even so the boiled pudding remained, along with the pie, a great and popular addition to the meal. The 18th and 19th centuries saw the continuation of the table centrepiece but this time they were readily devoured and designed to be eaten. Some were shaped like chariots or swans, some were even set pieces of a landscape or military helmets and all sculpted from nougats, ice creams, jellies and spun sugar. Simply breathtaking!

Cawdle

This delight remained popular from the 11th century right up to the reign of the Great Elizabeth. Although I think that I might find it a little boisterous for breakfast, as it was originally intended, but as a pudding served with whipped cream it's superb.

Ingredients:

Serves 4-6

- 3 cups of oats
- Honey
- Chopped dates or figs or both
- 2 cups of white wine
- 2 cups of cream
- Whipped cream
- Grated nutmeg

♠ Add your oats to a pan and stir in the wine. Cook together and gradually add the fruit.

♠ Stir in the honey to taste and cook for a further 5 minutes. Add the cream and cook for a further 5 minutes.

♠ Serve in individual dishes and top with whipped cream and grated nutmeg.

Why not top it all off with some cherries too? Quite a finish to a meal!

Chef's Tip

Soak your figs and dates in wine overnight. They will impart a superb flavour.

Strawberry & Peppercorn Pancakes

Now for a Victorian delight. The likes of the great Escoffier found these dishes a joy as they could be finished at the table. The final act makes a splendid climax for the dinner table. As a change, why not try red or green peppercorns?

Ingredients:

- 2 pancakes per person
- 1 tsp peppercorns
- 2oz (57g) butter
- 2oz (57g) sugar
- 2 tbs Grand Marnier
- 8oz (227g) strawberries

Chef's Tip

Warm your Grand Marnier before setting alight, it will ignite more easily.

♠ Crush half the peppercorns. Melt the butter in a frying pan. Add the sugar and crushed peppercorns. Keep the heat low and don't burn the sugar.

♠ Add the Grand Marnier and stir into the butter/peppercorn mix. Set it alight!

♠ As soon as the flames subside add the strawberries and toss them over to heat through for 30 seconds. Add the remaining peppercorns.

♠ Spoon the strawberries into the pancakes, sprinkle with caster sugar and top with thick cream.

This is pure decadence!

Raspberry Syllabub

A real favourite from the time of the Great Elizabeth. During the 16th century England rose to be one of the greatest powers on earth mainly, I believe, due to the influence of Elizabeth I ('Good Queen Bess') who ruled this nation for more years than many people lived!

This was the time of exploration, science, war with Spain and rotten teeth! Sugary foods were commonplace and I'm afraid it was actually fashionable to have bad teeth to show everyone that you could afford only the richest foods. Here is something a little different. Sweet and sugary yes but also absolutely heavenly as a light pudding and fabulous as a summer treat. This is one to take to Henley. During the 16th and 17th centuries a sweet white called Renish was available. You can still buy this now as any sweet wine from the Rhineland.

Ingredients:

Serves 6

- 8oz (227g) raspberries
- 2oz (57g) caster sugar
- 2 tbs rosewater, or lemon juice, or Kirsch
- ½ pint (237ml) double cream
- ½ pint (237ml) sweet white wine

Chef's Tip

Try not to wash soft fruits like raspberries and strawberries, it can make them very mushy. Just wipe them softly with kitchen towel.

A queen of puddings!

♠ Bruise half the raspberries in a bowl lightly with a wooden spoon, reserve the remaining berries and sprinkle them with a little of the rosewater/lemon juice/Kirsch.

♠ Beat the cream stiffly. Add the sugar and the wine and beat until the cream forms stiff peaks.

♠ Add 2 tbs of the cream to the berries, then add all the remaining berry mix to the cream.

♠ Fold the mix lightly so that the it is streaked with the colours of the berries and cream. Chill in a fridge for at least 2 hours.

♠ Serve in individual dishes and garnish with remaining raspberries.

Tart of Strawberries

Back in time to the 17th century again. Pies and tarts have always been a staple British food and this delight would have graced any table in the summer with its freshness and vibrant flavour.

Ingredients:

Serves 6

- 8oz (227g) of fresh strawberries, halved
- Shortcrust pastry (enough)
- 2oz (57g) sugar
- 2 tsp ground cinnamon
- 1 tsp ground ginger
- Whipped cream
- Brandy

Chef's Tip
Try making your own pastry and, if you wish, mixing the spices with the mixture.

♠ Roll out your pastry into a thin sheet. Cut the pastry in half and place your strawberries onto one of the pastry sheets. Top with the second sheet and close firmly.

♠ Egg-wash the pastry and sprinkle all over liberally with the sugar, cinnamon and ginger.

♠ Bake at 150°C for 15-20 minutes or until a deep golden brown.

♠ Cut into lozenges, allow to cool and serve with whipped cream that you have beaten with brandy.

A truly cavalier delight!

Christmas Pudding

This favourite has been with us for centuries. We first hear of rich fruit boiled puddings in the middle ages but this particular pudding has its origins in the early 18th century. The idea of spiced fruits in puddings goes back to the times when spicing was the only way to preserve fruit through the winter months. This has a particularly long list of ingredients, however, it's worth it. I promise you.

Ingredients:

Serves 6-8

- 1lb (453g) currants
- 1lb (453g) sultanas
- 1lb (453g) raisins
- 4oz (113g) mixed peel
- 4oz (113g) glacé cherries
- 4oz (113g) chopped almonds
- 1½lbs (680g) breadcrumbs
- 1lb (453g) grated carrot
- 1lb (453g) suet
- 2lbs (907g) brown sugar
- 8oz (227g) plain flour
- Rind and juice of 1 lemon
- Rind and juice of 1 orange
- 8 eggs
- ½ tsp salt
- 1 tsp mixed spice
- 1 tsp cinnamon
- 1 large bottle Guinness
- 1 cup of brandy
- ½ cup of rum

♠ Mix all the ingredients well together.

♠ Pack into three, 2 pint well-greased basins and cover with foil. Steam for 8 hours. If you are making 1 pint puddings steam for 6 hours.

♠ Make these puddings at least 4 months in advance and feed them with brandy each week until finally cooking to serve. Reheat by steaming for 1 hour.

Possibly the finest pudding recipe in the world!

Chef's Tip

When initially cooking the puddings check on the water levels, don't let the pan boil dry.

Real Mincemeat

Time for the mince pies! Many people don't realise that mincemeat is so named because it was originally made from pork. This is the original recipe and I think a super one. It has strong full flavours but remember that when this mix was made you wanted to show how well off you were. You over-spiced everything to impress your guests.

During the days after King Charles was executed Oliver Cromwell banned mince pies at Christmas as they used to be boat shaped and the lid was a small human figure. It was meant to be the child Christ in the manger and the puritans condemned this as idolatrous.

Ingredients:

Makes 36 pies

- 1lb (453g) minced pork
- 1lb (453g) dried fruit
- 2 tbs allspice
- 1 heaped tsp nutmeg
- 2 cups sugar
- Butter for cooking

Chef's Tip

Minced beef can be substituted. This mix freezes well but once made into pies consume within 3 days.

♠ Cook the mince through in a deep saucepan using a little butter. Add the sugar and spices.

♠ Cook for a further 15 minutes and add the fruit that you have been soaking overnight in brandy. Cook for a further 5 minutes.

♠ Prepare a suitable pastry – shortcrust or puff it's up to you. Bake at 180ºC for 35 minutes until golden brown.

♠ Top with whipped cream that you mixed with brandy.

Superbly seasonal!

Fried Pineapple with Ginger & Brandy

Another glimpse of the 18th century. Whereas this would have been plated up in the kitchen, you may wish to complete this dish at the table. The flavours of the pineapple and ginger are astonishing and work really well together.

We have had pineapples in Britain since the time of Elizabeth I. Her gardener was the famous John Tradescant and they finally managed to cultivate the pineapple here for the first time.

Ingredients:

Serves 4-6

- 1 large pineapple, peeled and diced
- 1 jar of stem ginger, sliced
- 3oz (85g) of butter
- 3oz (85g) of brown sugar
- 1 cup of brandy
- ½ pint (237ml) of double cream

Chef's Tip

The pineapple must be fresh; if you attempt to use tinned the dish will not work.

♠ In a large wok heat the butter. When really hot add the pineapple and cook for 5 minutes.

♠ Add the stem ginger and sugar and cook for a further 3-5 minutes or until the ingredients are softened.

♠ Now add the brandy and stir through well.

♠ Whilst hot serve and top with large helpings of the double cream either poured or whipped.

A real heart stopper!

Flaming Apple Flan

Again we have a dish from the Georgian time of the good Dr Johnson. This is really an indulgence in spices and brandy. The flavours are typical of the age and this makes a super pudding for a supper party with friends.

Ingredients:

Serves 4-6

- Enough shortcrust pastry to cover a good-sized flan dish
- Enough dessert apples to cover in 2 layers peeled, cored and sliced
- ½ cup of brown sugar or honey
- 1 tsp of allspice
- 1 tsp of cinnamon
- 1 tsp of grated nutmeg
- 1 orange for zesting
- Brandy

Chef's Tip

If using honey, monitor the cooking as honey can burn on occasion.

♠ Grease the flan case well and lay in your pastry. Lay in the apples to overlap and cover the pastry in 2 layers. You may also add some plums for extra flavour if you wish.

♠ Sprinkle with the sugar and then the spices. Cook in an oven at 180°C for 30 minutes or until cooked.

♠ Remove, allow to cool slightly and grate the orange zest over the surface.

♠ Now throw brandy all over the dish and ignite.

Pray for first aid!

Scrumplings

During the reign of Elizabeth I much was made of seasonal food, because there were no freezer lorries or chilled supermarket cabinets. During the autumn one of the treasures has always been the plum. Most varieties lend themselves superbly to this recipe. Clever use of marzipan too! The almond has always been a favourite for sweetmeats. Careful though, as almonds can really pile on the pounds. As well as actually having rotten teeth to show you could afford sweet things, some people even stained their teeth black in order to be fashionable. How bizarre!

Ingredients:

Serves 4-6

- 1lb (454g) shortcrust pastry
- 8 large plums
- 4oz (113g) marzipan
- Beaten egg and milk
- Cinnamon
- Brown sugar

Chef's Tip

Use some of the egg wash to seal the pastry corners as you fold them, they will adhere better.

♠ Roll out your pastry thinly and cut into squares.

♠ Stone your plums and replace the stone with a good large lump of marzipan.

♠ Put the plums in the centre of the pastry squares and fold in the corners to make a plum parcel.

♠ Place them in a well-greased dish and brush with beaten egg and milk and scatter well with cinnamon and brown sugar.

♠ Bake at 220ºC for 25 minutes.

A Tudor treat!

Ginger Pears

It's back to the days of the great Mrs Beeton for this one. This is the epitome of Victorian elegance and would look superb gracing any dinner or tea table.

Ingredients:

Serves 4-5.
(Scale down as you wish)

- 1½ (710ml) pints dry white wine
- ½ pint (237ml) of ginger wine
- 8oz (227g) caster sugar
- The juice and rind of 2 lemons
- 10 dessert pears
- Finely sliced stem ginger

Chef's Tip

If pouring more ginger wine over the dish when serving make sure it is warm. Don't lose the heat from the pears.

♠ Mix in a saucepan the wine, ginger wine, lemon juice and rind and gradually bring to the boil.

♠ Add the sugar and boil briskly for a few moments to produce a syrup.

♠ Place the pears in the pan and simmer gently for 20 minutes.

♠ Serve in shallow dishes with the syrup and fine slices of the stem ginger. Top with thick cream and more ginger wine if you wish.

A Victorian classic.

Rhubarb Mousse

A light pudding. What? Unbelievably, from the Elizabethan court a light and fluffy pudding ideal for summer. It is both refreshing and tasty. Rhubarb, like gooseberries, is not as common in greengrocers as it used to be. Ask for it, let's try to get it back in.

Ingredients:

Serves 6

- 1½lbs (680g) rhubarb
- 2oz (57g) of fine brown sugar
- 3 tsp gelatine
- 3 tsp lemon juice
- 4 eggs, separated
- 4oz (113g) caster sugar
- ½ pint whipping cream

Chef's Tip

Try to obtain the pink rhubarb if possible; it is ideal for this dish.

♠ Cook the rhubarb with the brown sugar and 4 tbs of water until the fruit is cooked. Allow the rhubarb to cool.

♠ Whilst cooling, in a separate bowl soften the gelatine in the lemon juice and 1 tbs of water.

♠ Whip the egg yolks and caster sugar and add to the rhubarb. Please note that the rhubarb should be cool but not cold.

♠ Whip until airy and frothy and then fold in the whipped egg whites and half of the whipped cream.

♠ Pour into serving glasses and top with broken ginger biscuits.

Super for an Ascot picnic.

West Country Lardy Buns

The idea of lardy buns, lardy cakes and dripping cakes (they are the same thing) has been with us for centuries. These cakes which are certainly not only filling but fattening are a delight from the kitchen. Originally the dripping was allowed to run on them from the spit on the meat jack by the open fire, and the cakes were cooked in front of the joint. Now we can allow ourselves the comfort of using the oven.

Ingredients:

Serves 4-6

- 6oz (170g) plain flour
- 1 tsp baking powder
- Pinch of salt
- 2oz (57g) of softened dripping
- 3oz (85g) of caster sugar
- 4oz (113g) sultanas
- Grated rind of ½ a lemon
- 1 egg
- 2 tbs milk
- Butter for greasing

♠ Sift the flour, salt and baking powder into a bowl. Rub in the dripping until you get to the breadcrumb stage.

♠ Blend in the other dry ingredients. Mix together the egg and milk and add it to the dough.

♠ Spoon the mixture into well-greased bun tins and bake at 180°C for about 25 minutes.

♠ Serve whilst warm, with cream if you are feeling brave.

A Christmas treat!

Chef's Tip

Beef dripping is the best for this dish; you may use pork but some find it cloys a little.

Somerset Apple Cake

All the apple-producing counties had their own recipes for cakes made from local produce, Somerset was no exception. This recipe comes from the area around Glastonbury where apples have been grown in abundance for centuries. This cake would have found its way into the refectory of its great abbey on many occasions and been a delight to the abbot and monks during meal times. Now it's just perfect tea.

Ingredients:

Serves 4-6

- 3oz butter
- 6oz caster sugar
- Grated rind of 1 orange
- 8oz (227g) self-raising flour
- 1lb (454g) Bramley apples, peeled, cored and cubed
- 2 beaten eggs
- 3tbs milk
- 2oz (57g) chopped candied peel
- 1tbs (453g) granulated sugar

♠ Pre-heat the oven to 180ºC.

♠ Cream together the butter, sugar and orange rind. Add your eggs, flour and milk. Gently add your apple cubes and fold in well.

♠ Place your mix into a well-greased tin about 9 inches (23cm) across.

♠ Sprinkle with sugar and bake for 45 minutes or until cooked.

I like it hot with cream.

Chef's Tip

Be gentle when adding your apples. Over stirring too roughly will break up the apple cubes.

Baked & Frosted Apples

This is originally a Tudor dish but it was later modified by the great Escoffier. It makes use of mincemeat. See our previous recipe to get the best result.

Ingredients:

Use 1 apple per person. Russets are superb for this dish.

Serves 4

- 4 apples
- 4oz (113g) mincemeat
- 2 egg whites, whipped
- Caster sugar

Chef's Tip

If you do not have a Chef's blowtorch simply remove the apples from the oven after 15 minutes, spoon on the meringue and replace in the oven at 220°C for the remaining cooking time or until the meringue is deep gold.

♠ Core but do not peel each apple. Fill the cavity two thirds full with the mincemeat.

♠ Using your egg whites and sugar make a meringue mixture.

♠ Bake the apples at 180°C for 20 minutes or until cooked.

♠ Spoon the meringue over the apples and flash them with a chef's blowtorch.

♠ You may then serve with whipped brandy cream.

A Christmas treat!

Plum Flan

A friend of mine sent me this recipe as one from the fens. Like all seasonal fruit, plums are greatly prized when fresh and available. This dish seems to date from the 19th century and employs an interesting mix of yoghurt and soured cream. It makes for a splendid sharp flan. Although I get the distinct impression that the original Victorian recipe would have had curds instead of yoghurt and soured cream.

Ingredients:

Serves 4-6

- 6oz (170g) sweet shortcrust pastry
- 1lb (454g) halved stoned plums
- ¼ pint (118ml) soured cream
- ¼ pint (118ml) plain yoghurt
- 1oz (28g) caster sugar
- 3 egg yolks
- ½ tsp mixed spice
- 2oz (57g) brown sugar
- 1 tsp cinnamon

Chef's Tip
To obtain a good crust increase the heat of the oven to 220°C for the last 5 minutes of baking.

♠ Beat together the cream, yoghurt, caster sugar, egg yolks and spices.

♠ Pour the mixture into a deep flan dish. Arrange the plums with their cut side facing up on the pastry mix and bake at 200°C for 20 minutes.

♠ Remove from the oven and sprinkle with the cinnamon and brown sugar, return to the oven and bake for a further 20 minutes.

♠ Serve with lashings of custard.

Hot Cross Buns

The hot cross bun has been a part of our Easter celebrations since Pontius was a pilate. Its genet spiced flavour and mix of fruits is perfect for the occasion. Traditionally the buns you eat on Good Friday should be baked on that day, it was long considered bad luck to eat them before Easter. I shudder to think what our ancestors would have made of supermarkets stocking them from January!

Ingredients:

Serves 6 (makes 18 buns)

- 1lb (454g) plain flour sifted well, divided into 2 bowls
- 1oz (28g) fresh yeast
- 1 tsp sugar
- ½ pint (237ml) mixed warm milk and water
- 1 tsp cinnamon
- 1 tsp grated nutmeg
- ½ tsp allspice
- ½ tsp salt
- 2oz (57g) caster sugar
- 4oz (113g) currants
- 1oz (28g) chopped or melted butter
- 1 beaten egg

Chef's Tip

When proving your dough, a warm dry place is good. Perhaps an airing cupboard?

♠ Blend together the yeast with a little of the water/milk mix, allow to work and when it froths add the rest of the liquid. Add this into one of the bowls of flour and mix well.

♠ Cover the bowl and leave to prove for 45 minutes.

♠ In the second bowl of flour add the fruit, spices, salt and sugar. Then add the butter and egg and mix with the risen dough from the first bowl.

♠ Knead this well with your hands and leave to stand for at least 1 hour.

♠ Divide your mix into 18 buns and cut a cross on the surface of each. Leave for 20 minutes before placing in an oven and baking at 220ºC for 20 minutes.

♠ Make a syrup from 2 tbs sugar boiled with 2 tbs milk and brush this on the buns hot from the oven. Allow to cool.

Just spread with butter, nothing else is necessary.

Figgy Pudding

A celebratory treat from the 15th century. This rich fruity pudding was traditionally eaten on or near Palm Sunday, which was sometimes known as 'fig Sunday' owing to the fact that figs were commonly eaten on that day.

It is similar in many ways to the Christmas pudding but the quantity of figs gives an individual flavour.

Ingredients:

Serves 6-8

- 8oz (227g) dried sliced figs
- 4oz (113g) raisins
- 8oz (227g) dates, stoned and sliced
- 4oz (113g) sliced stem ginger
- 4 tbs rum
- 6oz (170g) white breadcrumbs
- 8oz (227g) self-raising flour
- 6oz (170g) shredded suet
- ½ tsp salt
- 3 eggs
- Grated rind and juice of 1 lemon
- Milk, a little

Chef's Tip

Always ask your butcher for suet, it is a natural by-product of the meat. It will be fresher than from a store.

♠ Allow your fruit and ginger to soak in a bowl with the rum overnight.

♠ Mix the breadcrumbs, flour, salt and suet together. Beat the eggs well and blend them into the dry ingredients.

♠ Add the lemon rind, juice and the fruit. Mix this well and don't forget to add the rum that the fruit has been soaking in.

♠ Pour this into a well-greased pudding basin, about 2 pint (946ml) capacity. Steam for 4 hours.

♠ Serve with lots of cream whipped with more rum.

More adult than an Easter egg!

Royal Gingerbread

Now for a real treat. A shortbread recipe that dates from the restoration of King Charles II in 1660. This simple but superb recipe is magnificent as a biscuit and just as good when served with strawberries and cream. In the 17th century it was common for these gingerbreads to be baked in gilded tins, hence the saying 'gilt off the gingerbread'.

Ingredients:

Serves 4-6

- 4oz (113g) plain flour
- 3oz (85g) caster sugar
- ½oz (14g) ground ginger
- 2 egg yolks
- 1 egg white
- Caraway seeds to taste

Chef's Tip
Grease your baking tray well with butter for these biscuits. They will turn out better.

♠ Mix together the flour, sugar, ginger and egg yolks to a smooth paste.

♠ Roll out to about ¼ in thick. Cut into the shapes as you wish and lay them on a greased baking tray.

♠ Bake at 160ºC for about 15-20 minutes, (They should get to a light gold colour).

♠ After 10 minutes of cooking, sprinkle with the caraway seeds and return for the remaining cooking time.

Perfect for a royal occasion.

A Fond Farewell...

Well there you have it. I hope you have enjoyed this little trip through the centuries and peeping in on the tables of our ancestors. Cooking is a passion both for the Chef and myself. Allow me to thank you for purchasing this book and joining us on our journey.

For further reading, you might like to consider taking the following three wonderful tomes to bed ...

A Heritage of British Cooking by Maggie Black
In fact any book by Ms Black is superb.

Around the Roman Table by Patrik Faas
A first-rate book, magnificently researched.

The Epicurean by Charles Ranhofer
A true classic.

You may also have wondered what goes on behind the scenes during a photo shoot for a cookery book such as this. Well, I hope the following few pages will enlighten you a little and make you smile. We had an enormous amount of fun!

Behind the Scenes...

Waiter! There's a hare in my sandwich

Flambéing - Chef's way

'Kissing the eel' – an old Lichfield tradition

Look! It's still wriggling!

The Prof explains about the Glory Hole Oven

Every chef should be well hung!

Ha! You've found the chilli-flavoured chocolate!

Chef's wife, Alison, holds her sacrifice aloft

If you need fresh apples - send
Chef up a tree

Getting up was the
easy part!

Trying to make a fish in a bag
look sexy

Blackbrook Antiques - a
dream location for period shots

Thrales Restaurant
40-44 Tamworth Street
Lichfield Staffordshire WS13 6JJ
Tel 01543 255091

Thrales has been run as a restaurant with Simon Smith as chef for the past 21 years. It was originally 3 cottages and an abattoir with a butcher's shop onto the high street. There are still many of the features remaining and the building has a unique character with a wealth of beams and private tables in nooks and crannies. The food reflects the history of England as well as a modern diversity of European dishes with menus changing on a regular basis. Thrales is also a showcase for the dishes in this book and has been the location of much of the food photography. For further details visit www.thrales.co.uk.

First Course

*Pan fried calf sweetbreads with a cream & sherry sauce, pancetta
Faggot from the butcher at Barton Marina with an onion gravy
Pan fried king prawns with a lemon & saffron sauce
Breaded, deep fried goat's cheese with fresh plum & pine kernel salad
Deep fried pork in a crispy batter with mango & spring onion
Grilled local black pudding & chorizo sausage
*Sardines stuffed with nuts

Main Course

Rib of Scotch beef with Béarnaise sauce & Yorkshire pudding
Slow braised free range belly pork, crackling & orange sauce
*Sauté of lamb with Jerusalem artichoke, broad beans & saffron
*Saddle of Black Forest wild boar, wrapped in pancetta
*Pan fried calf liver with smoked bacon & capers
Roast, stuffed saddle of hare with red wine sauce, pancetta & mushrooms
*Baked trout with almonds & ale

Pudding

*Elizabethan rhubarb mousse with shortbread
Bread & butter pudding with vanilla whipped cream
Traditional treacle tart with custard & whipped cream
Vanilla pannacotta with a plum & Autumn berry compote
Poached orange in a honey & Cointreau syrup
Vanilla crème brulée with fresh raspberries
A terrine of dark Belgian chocolate with crushed meringue & almonds

* Denotes a recipe taken from this book

Culinary Historian - Professor Roland Rotherham

Professor Roland Rotherham started his life at a very early age and was educated to a fair standard at numerous schools that mysteriously burned down shortly before his departure. Whilst still a young man he decided to enter the army (much to their chagrin) and ended up serving in the cavalry, seeing much of his service as a member of the personal staff of Her Majesty Queen Elizabeth II.

Travelling extensively with HM, The Professor enjoyed experiencing the cultures of the various countries he visited and noted down many of their customs, beliefs and, of course, recipes – gathering over 1,500 in India alone! Before being impeached for treason Professor Rotherham

had been seconded to King Hussein of Jordan, Emperor Haille Selassie and The Nizam of Hyderabad, to name but a few, who benefited from his expertise in protocol and mixing martinis.

A frequent broadcaster on radio and television, The Professor is currently ranked third in the world for his expertise on The Holy Grail and The Spear of Destiny. He was once described by BBC broadcaster Malcolm Boyden as "A national treasure and one of Britain's best kept secrets".

Master Chef - Simon Smith

Simon has had a varied, worldwide culinary career. He did his training in Switzerland and then Paris. From there he moved on to London and worked as chef saucier at The Inn on the Park in Park Lane. Whilst there he worked on the wedding of the Shah of Persia. In addition Smith has helped create a Japanese buffet for 1,500 in London, a Jewish wedding in New York for 4000 and worked at The British Embassies in both Paris and Vienna.

Simon has appeared on several TV shows and was a regular on the Carlton Food network. He has also appeared on television in Lyon and Bologna. He has done many cookery demonstrations throughout Europe to promote British food.

He is currently chef/patron of Thrales Restaurant in Lichfield, Staffordshire where he has been for the past twenty years. He has also been heavily involved in a twinning agreement with the Toques Blanches Lyonnaise.

Simon has won many prizes for his craft including three gold medals at Salon Culinaire competitions throughout the UK, The Tudor France Award for Contribution to the Hotel and Catering Industry and achieved Thrales's Michelin rating.

Photographer – Sophie Overend

Sophie's interest in photography developed when she was at university studying fashion and where, in her final year, she specialised in Fashion Marketing and Advertising.

She has worked as a photographer for nearly four years, starting as a Nightlife Photographer in Birmingham for www.tilllate.com. Sophie has worked in some of the biggest nightclubs in Birmingham – *Miss Moneypenny's*, *Air* and *Radius* to name but a few and she is also the resident photographer for *Bloc Beatz* and *Simma*.

Sophie has also photographed many weddings and has created promotional shots for models, clothing and shoe companies. Recently she had the pleasure of photographing Rolf Harris and other artists such as Henderson Cisz and Doug Hyde.

She now also has the wonderful experience of photographing food for this book, which, she says, has been a sheer delight!

Thanks...

To my comrade Simon Smith, hereafter called 'The Chef' for being professional, talented, an absolute hoot and so damned good! And not forgetting dear Carol his formidable sous chef.

Of course, to Adrian Jackson of the Lichfield Garrick for making this book possible and to all the staff of the Garrick for their kindness and hard work during our performances.

To Sophie Overend for her excellent photography, a true artist.

Also to my friends Stefan Struik and Pieter Bakker for their unswerving encouragement and to Loes and Cees Hoppezak for their hospitality and endless supply of Dutch lubrication.

To 'Auntie' June Semple whose sausage rolls could seduce an empire.

A special mention to Chris Shute a great 'trencherman' to whom the puddings section is dedicated.

Index